(MY TRIALS MY TRIBULATIONS)

(ONLY BY THE GRACE OF GOD)

Author: Crystal Evans

Dedication

       I want to first dedicate this book to God, for allowing me to be a part of this lifetime. I thank him for not only the blessings and good things that happened, I also thank him for the bad things, because not only did he bring me out of them they helped to strengthen me. God pulled me through, and without me going through the storms that I have experienced through my life. I would not have gained the wisdom, knowledge, and understanding that I have today. Most Importantly, I would not be able to help others that may feel like giving up on life. To the readers "You can do it", I am here to encourage you.

I thank you Lord for telling me to write this book, cause by doing so, it brought me healing, and made it possible for me to forgive. I thank you for keeping me in the wilderness in my dry season, while I have been yet trying to find me. Learning how to love myself, and falling in love with you. Crying out countless nights from being so hurt. I felt ripped into shreds, but you put me back together. Lord you forgave me, I thank you Lord for allowing me to go through and come out so I can lead your people back to you.

I thank you Lord that through it all you had kept me, embraced me, healed me, and provided for me, when I could not provide for myself and now, God I will lift you up for the rest of my days. I will be your living example, an agent in the earth. I am sorry Lord, for taking so long to write this book, when you told me to get it done and provided me with the time. I let my emotions and feeling get the best of me, while you said people were dying prematurely. Forgive me, for allowing myself to get in your way, you said this book will bring healing and deliverance to those who read so let your healing go forth. I thank you for using me Lord: a willing-vessel.

I want to thank my family for giving me something to write about. Just kidding; but for loving me, spending time with me and enjoying life with me. By being living examples, showing me the world by just living your lives, it helped to push me even harder in life. Big ma and Granddad, thank you for always believing in me, and to all my best friends' forever (bff's). I want to thank: the Carter's & family, as well as Rock of Deliverance ministries, Monisa Johnson, for taking me in and loving me as her own, I really appreciate you. Dr. Patience Adisheda, for showing me love and performing surgeries and seeing me when I could not afford medical practices, and unlike any other doctor, you seen something in me and also you had talked to me and prayed for me and with me. Thank you woman of God, you preformed over 6,000.00 in services free of charge. To the other women who poured into my life and has been good friends Katrina, Tunisia, Tamika, Ms. Kay, Tyressa, Patrice, Danielle, Tasha go, Colentha, Semone, Latonya, Suga Wuga, Monie, Tatay, Carlita, TT, Vonda, Olivia, Lolita, My Certified Nurse Aides (CNA) sisters, the Brown family, my Pastor and Co-Pastor Clearance & Robyn Langston who showed me an illustration of how life is supposed to be and gave love and instructions from God and my Word in Action family (W.I.A.). I love you and everyone whom I met or came across thus far and those whom I will meet in the days to come; my 5th grade teacher Janice Stewart who poured into me spiritually telling me about spirits that inter the body through sex at age 11, a wonderful woman of God, I love you as well thank you readers for reading this book... May God bless you and keep as well as lead you on your journey...

Journey

From a child into a woman; since conceived from her mother's wombs, Crystal life's journey, followed by tragedies, lost loved ones and those who had disparaging attitudes- loss of innocence, God's impeccable grace and mercy preceded every outcome. Because of her alacrity to follow after a righteous God, Crystal has found what most of us take 40 years to find and that is, "the peace of God that surpasses all of our understanding", to go through trials after trials and still standing after all, says it all! Ever since her youth and into adult life her magnanimous character still draws and touches the hearts of every young and elderly. This book will take you through many emotional- provoking events, but understand one thing as you read, you will be reading the testimonies and truth that she overcame by the power of the Most High God. Her soft spot for the living, and the creation of God, and creator will exemplify her ideology through the texts of each page. At last, Crystal has finally shared what the world has been waiting for, "simplicity" in the rawest form! Positively, loving energy that God had given her to spread wildly in the heart of people such as you and me. Allow Crystal's fire to burn into each of your hearts as you witness in words her truths.

…Anonymous friend…

To my wonderful friend, Crystal Smith- Evans, you are a kind hearted woman that tries to always do the right thing even if sometimes it may conflict with your heart. You are one of the strongest, craziest, and determined woman that I know, nothing holds you back nor breaks you. When you had fallen, you were able to get back up. I have shared some of my most memorable and wildest moments with you, I love you and that will never change, you are more than a friend, you are my sister.

Semone Newsome

I first had the pleasure of meeting Crystal Evans about 4 years ago. When we met it was definitely God-Ordained. Crystal was in a very trying time in this period of her life. I was in a position where God had set me up to be a blessing to her by providing what she needed at that time in her life. We met at church Word in Action Christian Center in Detroit, MI. I must say for myself meeting Crystal was a complete turnaround blessing in me and my family's lives as well. She had the Spirit of an Angel. A very selfless, warm, sweet, faith-filled woman of God. Omg, her faith and endurance, and tenacity is what stood out the most to me. Her faith ministered to my Spirit upon us having countless interactions and fellowships. Sometimes, I'd be blown away by the strength this Woman of God possessed. She always smiled thru her pain no matter what. As time went on and our relationship in Christ developed, she began to open up about her past life. This young lady pressed, praised, and overcame many obstacles in her life. I could never figures out how she'd still be standing in the mist of her desert. But truly I know it had to take the hand of our Almighty God to keep this mighty woman afloat. What an Awesome God we Serve!! I'm blessed to have crossed paths with Crystal (middle name??) Evans!! Hallelujah!!

Kiya Williams

You've always been such a great friend, sis and confidant never judging me and always willing to help me, no matter what you're naturally one of a kind, and handle everything with grace as a God fearing woman should. I think God put you in my life for a reason, before I met you I had no self-respect and low self-esteem now I at least try to take care of myself and do a good job at it, and no one can call me ugly and I take them seriously, and I'll always have you to thank for that, I love you sis 4 life

Jessicia Russell

When I first met crystal was at the rock of deliverance church in Champaign IL having her at this church my girls and I was like having a new generation anointing in my life that I could relate to. Crystal is very spiritual and highly motivated. Whatever goals she makes she will accomplish which gives me motivation to put God first. Crystal has so many talents from singing, praise dancing, cooking, being a beautician, doing make up, and praying warrior, intercessor, writer, teacher, wife and a good friend. May God continue to guide you and you keep being a positive impact on everyone that meet you love you and thank you

Tameka Williams

I'm so proud to have you as a sister and a friend. You are a very beautiful, strong, loving, and caring woman. With all that you have been through you continue to triumph and I so appreciate your willingness and honesty in sharing your story with the world. What a brave soul you are an inspiring woman for all woman young and old. I love you forever and always your sister/friend
Patrice Anderson

Crystal is my heart and my one and only best friend she can be a little crazy, goofy, outspoken, and lovable all at once but at the end of the day I love her to pieces she is one of the strongest women I know and I've been blessed to have her apart of my life for 25 years
Tyreesa Lang

Introduction

This is a story about pain, transition and triumphs. A thorough story about recovering from past hurts, conveying it through clarity, while being able to transition into a position of growth. Happiness does not just happen overnight, it happens when you make the decision to just be happy. This story is inspired by my life, my trials and tribulations, the things that embarrassed me and I was ashamed to have done. Most of all, I am writing this book to let you know that I have been through the things that you went through or that some of you are going through and that you are not alone. No more stuff held in that needs to be released, no more secrets the inner me desires to hide because of the Fear {False +Evidence+ Appearing+ Real= Fear} that I held inside, I had to release these things so that I could become healed. If you slip and fall and it produces a wound most times the wound hurts and need to be healed.

Nevertheless, when things start to happen to us, most of the time we appear to be substantial, we disguise our feelings to hide up the pain. We began to do other things that we believe can take the pain away, trying to avoid the healing process, because we do not want to go through it which we will one day have to deal with, so why put it off? So let's take the time to heal it. God is the only one that can heal, we cannot do it on our own, and this book will strengthen, and even encourage you, bringing to your understanding a closer relationship with God. Letting you know when you cannot,

God can. It will also bring to you healing and deliverance and show you how to deal with life differently, and you will gain and understand love; learn how to let go and let God so that you may follow his will, and not your own obtaining that "now faith" with patience, clarity, knowledge, wisdom and understanding, not only in your life but in the things of the Lord. When you look at me, what do you see? Look at the cover of this book do you see a young lady that was lost, confused, unable to love? And did not love herself? Do you see a young lady that continued to put herself in dangerous situations? Being raped multiple times, and kidnaped, doing what I had to do to live, full of anguish and pain, unable to say no to sex so, nevertheless, ended up with male and female sex partners. Going to "hell on a sky rocket", was my destined place. Or do you just see a nice young lady with a nice little shape? I was full of hell and full of sinful living, by the things of this world blaming my life and the things that happened to me on others. We must all go through some things, and I had no right to make any excuses because of some things I had consequently put myself in, by making unwise decisions or lazy ones, just trusting the wrong people. In this present day we must cover our children and cover ourselves. You might ask how you establish a covering. "Knock, seek, and ask the Lord and build a solid relationship with him, dwell in his shadows; then will you be protected.

    This is just an introduction of what the book will be about. Read it and do not feel sorry for me, just apply it to your life, on how to change your situations. Some things are going to bring out your joy and bring out some the pain, but the Lord told me to let you know my story, so here it is. After I write this, some people are not going to like me, some will even judge me, but I do not care, I am following the orders of the Lord. I am sorry for the things that I have done, I have already repented to my Lord and Savior Jesus Christ and I now have no pain nor shame just truth and I have to tell. You may believe you know me, but you have no idea. You might recognize the facts about me or some of the things that took place in my life but you do not know me. You know how it is when you think you found "that one", which you want to spend all of your time with them and falling in love, oh you want to talk to them all day long and to be in their presence while you feel all crazy inside.

To know a person, you must seek after that person. Then, you began to build a relationship, and then you communicate with the person to understand more about them. You cannot just be on the outside looking in, it takes time, patience and learning, you can not only just like what they like, and pick out of their dis-likes –learn what makes them upset, what makes them happy. When we spend some time, it put forth effort; we want to know how they think and see certain things, this is how I feel as far as family members and friends, however, they cannot tell you how you are supposed to see life or even if you are hurting and also how God feels. When other's claim to know my heart, only God knows because he designed it and created me. Reading a person is not knowing the person. People say "that he say, she say "without knowing for themselves - they want to speak the bible but never picked it up, they go by what they have heard. According to the book of Proverbs. We must "teach a child in the way he/she may go in, so that they will never depart from it", so what are you teaching your children parents? Consequently, if you do not teach them the right way they will never know what is right or wrong. Children/teenagers/young adults, if the parents/guardians, do not teach you in the things God had entrusted within your caretaker, find him (God) on your own because when you seek God and his right ways, all things that you run after shall come after you. The bible says that "we all are sinners", so who can we judge? Basically no one! And how can we put so much time into getting to know another individual, and do not get to know God, and follow his commandments? Or at least try? If you do not know God's love, you cannot truly love; it will not be genuine. True love keeps no records of wrongs and it does not get you back later for the hurts and the pains that you have caused.

    At different times in my life, I put "nouns" before God, people places or things like; that man I loved so much, I forgot to wake up and pray to God, because I woke up thinking about him or how I can make him feel good "him, him, him" or partying when I knew I had to go to church the following morning and could not get up due to being out too late -the things that I have said or done, that was contrary to the word of God, it was what I felt like doing. Moreover, when we think it is all about us putting ourselves first instead of God, which some of us are still doing until we get into trouble, and who the first one we call? How can we call on him in our troubled times and not love on him when we are not in the troubled times? It is like we are using him but he (God) is no fool and then you will get mad when he (God) do not show up when you need him to, and then you want a saint to pray, going around asking someone else to do what you could do for yourself if you just had a relationship with him (God) he will never cheat on you, nor change his mind about you or do anything to hurt you or even hate on you - just to love you, help you and heal you, never will he count you out.

    Most days I cry out for our youth feeling the pain they are feeling. The trials that they are currently enduring; they live through it daily as it worsens. We should know, because we were once youth ourselves, but since those past years, things have only started to become worse. Due to the hidden secrecy, such as rape, lack of communication, none family values, lack of having a two parent home- seeing the example of a true man, being the head of household and a wife that is faithful to serving. When a wife submits to her husband and children it will serve the family by bringing peace and God's love; no stress can enter in. For example, I have been a wife for 7 years so I can tell you about being a wife because I lived it as well as being a child, taking up the role of servant. When it comes to the men, we are to pray for them; it keeps the household together and without this order the household will fail. For example, I had once been the child of a broken home, and if you do not have that equal love (chastening), that corrects you in your wrong doings, to help make your path sufficient through life, that supports you to do good (correction), if there is no chastening, you will fall for anything. If love is the thing that we lack, we will tend to look for it in bad habits, sex or relationships, thinking a non-spouse/spouse can fill that void of love that we are supposed to feel from our parents as children. One should not only be told about love by words alone, but to demonstrate it (love) as well. That is how hurt and pain form (lack of knowing God's love). How could one know about God's love and healing? If no one ever told us that, and if they have told us, they did not tell us how to receive God's love and healing; however, we cannot play the blame game, or use excuses. This is why the youth are being corrupted and desensitized to love – TV, videos media etc.

    Moreover, the truth is: it starts at home; home is where healing and growing takes place, a place to nurture a situation, but you must do all things with grace and love as you treat yourself, be gentle and kind, not judgmental but give factual information and discipline. Because they are the future (grace and love). The enemy comes to steal kill and to destroy, devouring what we allow him to devour, and in this case it's our youth. We as people parish because of the lack of knowledge. So take the time to teach, talk, and build a relationship with others and let them know your story. In sense, some of the same things that happened to you may have happened to others. It may have been a different way, but let them know that you care and that every situation has a way out, and pay attention to them and make them feel comfortable to come to you; do not ignore, being a parent is a job! You've had that child now, so take care of it. Its over for the partying and living life care free now, you have a responsibility, so let's get it together to fix our situations because it is not only nationwide, it's also worldwide. Also, we must protect them (our youth) because there are some sick people out here in the world, that enjoy hurting others, most of them prey on children, so know where they are going, so many children/young adults come up missing because they do what they want to do and go where they want to go. Our foundation should be the word of God, so let's make a safer world. For instance, some people do not like others dress so they fight or jump on one another or if you are in a relationship and your boyfriend cheats on you, now without cause the females are into an disagreement, and do not even know each other, but mad from the pain that was caused. So do get mad at the other woman for not knowing. When you might have so much in common to help one another.

    Do not permit yourself to grow hatred from a negative experience. We as people, or couples definitely need to alter the way we deal with things in our spirits. Let's pray about it, for instance, I lived both lives and both were fun, but the way I am living now is a more peaceful way and I gained more understanding as I grew. Many people hated on me throughout my life, family, friends, boyfriends and people who I do not even know and it is worse because of the favor that God placed upon my life. Each and every day we are given a chance to build a relationship with God, which is how favor is obtained. Since I now have given back my life to him (God) this was a choice I willingly had made. You can choose to; as I looked back over my life and I think of all the things God pulled me from, there was no way out, that is how I know it is a true and living God that keeps and protects me from all danger. Therefore God is real. No, one cannot convince me that he does not exist. But from my life experiences which was a true struggle, maybe some of you can relate, but if you do not believe in God, you have not seen God work at first- hand. Maybe your situation has not come yet, the word of the Lord says, "every knee shall bow and every tongue shall confess Jesus is Lord". I want to finish by saying, do not feel sorry for me, I am no longer a victim, I am a champion, and "I can do all things through Christ who strengthens me". He turned my mess into a lesson, test into a testimony, and my trial into triumph, mistakes are not meant to be looked down upon, especially if a person has messed up badly, we must ask God for forgiveness, and forgive our debtors as we have been forgiven of our transgressions, and love, but most importantly learning how to keep God first and foremost, because doing this; what can stand against you? Nothing.

Prayer:

Lord God you are: awesome, amazing, wonderful, marvelous, gracious, lovely, worth, magnificent, you are king of kings, Lord of Lords, victorious, you are everything to me. I love you with all of my being. I thank you Lord for all things, without you there would be nothing, including me. I would be nothing but filthy rags, which I am, that has been cleaned up by you. You are worthy of all honor, glory, and praise. I will show your people back to you, not me. You gave me this book. I thank you for using me, to heal, deliver and set free through you. It has not been easy being pressed down, but to whom much is given more is required. Lord continue to use me not only in my family, spiritual and natural, but in this entire earth. I am ready and the fear is gone, I am ready to go up Lord, I thank you for all the people that helped me along this journey and poured into my life. It made me a woman of God. Your word helped clean me up to look like you Lord, and saving me and others through me. I am chosen by you and nobody or anything can change that; even when I felt left out because they did not choose me you were protecting me hiding me and keeping me. Preparing me for my time, my season and the overflow, I thank you that my cup is running over. I am walking in all of my blessings because I stood on your promises. You granted me my gifts, no more hold ups or obstacles holding me back. I will leap for joy as you promote me. I will take off like a rocket and soar past the limits of the sky. I will forever chase after you, thank you Lord for the multi-million dollar deals and movies and TV shows, plays, business, jobs for family and me being able to help change this world with your instructions. Thank you Lord God that I will never need or want for anything and that my enemies are no longer enemies, because you can change the hearts of men towards me. And now I will teach them about forgiveness and love, leading all souls back to you. You are the one and only love of my life, you are worthy of all my praises Lord. I have to bless you. It is my will to praise your Holy name, In Jesus name Amen.

I am somebody because I am a child of God

WHERE'S MY MOTHER

Journey

Sitting in the second row in a pew with my grandmother hugging me, squeezing tightly, as if she was holding on for dear life. The music started to come from the piano and as I looked to the right of her, I saw all of her children present except for my mother. My aunt and uncles sat waiting patiently for the service to begin, as I drifted off into space, and all I could remember was me, going into "la, la," land. All I could envision was the good times playing UNO, Checkers; memory, we would lay in the bed and cycle our legs starting from slow to fast until we got tired and then we would hug and laugh. Playing pity pat, going to the zoo, shed aquarium, out to eat, shopping, or just spending quality time cooking, talking and cleaning. Shaken from memory, I was distracted and was forced back to reality by a lady who approached us, asking if our family would move up to the first row. At this time I began to look around for my mother, but I was unable to find her. I started to get upset because I really wanted my mother to be here with me, l and trying to think about the good times only made things worse. "Ahhhhhhhhh", I started to scream trying to hold back the tears by holding my breath; didn't work, all that did was made me dizzy and unable to breath. As the room started to spin and the walls started to close in, everyone looked at me not fully knowing what to do, a few people grabbed me and walked me out into the hall. Trying to find a bathroom to muffle the sound of my voice, more people came in the ladies room asking me if I was ok, telling me they were sorry for my loss. I heard voices but didn't pay attention to the faces I felt like passing out from being so overwhelmed.

Journey

I continued crying, asking them "where is my mom, I want my mom, I need her!" Two of my sisters came in and started hugging me assuring me that it would be ok, but it wasn't, because my mother was lying in a box, not moving and not here with me. I needed her to hug me. Reality had finally kicked in that she was dead. I was still in shock from the day they told me. I was getting dressed for school and the telephone started ringing when my aunt answered the phone and called me into the room. She was so insensitive; "Crystal, your Mother died! Go get Suga Wuga from school she went to breakfast". So, I ran out of the house, but before I could get across the street, I looked at the school and my mother's face flashed before me. I stopped running and started crying in the middle of the street I dropped to my knees and the disciplinarian came out to grab me before a car could hit me. He pulled me inside the office where people gathered around me asking me what happened. All I told them was that my mom was gone and I continued to weep.

Trying to find ways to delete her from my memory and act as though these things never took place; telling myself, "you never had a mother so how can you remember someone that was never there or something that was never true, they are not memories", I told myself. It is just a movie. Year after year I tried more and more to believe this, but it became hard for me around Mother's Day or when someone would say man, "that's Crystal" Tisa's daughter! She looks just like her, and then I would remember her and then I would start to get angry, and basically start to hate the person that gave the compliment, because at this time I didn't see it as a compliment, I didn't want to know her, it hurt me too bad to think about anything concerning her. The memories, good and bad I was trying to mask myself from the pain by covering up the facts of reality. Crying and screaming inside but I smiled like everything was cool. I just needed a hug or someone to talk to, but everyone was busy with a life of their own, I was invisible. I started to form a new world (fantasy Island) of make believe or a place where I can chose to believe what I want. Which made it able for me to cope with life and not feel so suicidal because I just wanted to end it all; just to be with my mom.

Flipping through some old pictures, I came across a photo of her big radiant smile where it looked like she didn't have a care in the world. I woke up crying this was only a dream. I missed her and I was trying to fight the feeling desperately. The birds were chirping and the fresh air came rushing in. I got out of bed and walked around the house. Breakfast was made, it was bacon, eggs, toast and grits. What I really wanted was cereal instead, honeycombs with slushy milk. After eating breakfast, Bigma took me into the bathroom and washed me up, scrubbing every nook and cranny. She scrubbed my face so hard it turned red, but I'm brown skinned. She said she was "making me clean". She would get me dressed and I would go out and run errands with her and Granddad to the candy store warehouse, out to lunch with friends, doctors' appointments or to visit family members. Must not forget shopping of course, riding with them in the Cadillac It was like I was riding a magic carpet. Anything I wanted, they bought. Some said I was spoiled rotten, others didn't really care. I would sing and dance and they would show me off to their friends. I had on my little Kentsetta dress, baby doll ruffle socks and pretty bows on my shoes. Any song that came on the radio I knew it and I sang it. Sometimes my uncle would play the piano and I would sing. Everybody loved me... well, mostly everybody.

Well to make a long story short my auntie was very jealous of me hated the point of my existence, I mean couldn't stand me. She felt I took her sister away, when my mother choose to have me, and after I was born she felt I had too much attention. Her grandparents, my great-grandparents praised me "Crystal, Crystal, Crystal" was what they would say, "she's so polite, can sing and dance, she's so cute, says please and thank you, just so sweet and respectful has great manners." My auntie possessed some of the same qualities but no one acknowledged her because of her rotten attitude, so she held it against me. She could sing and dance as well, but just didn't get the same praise. Before I was born, my mother was everyone's favorite and my aunt just wanted the spotlight but could never steal the show. It was always "TC" can cook and make sure the house was clean. She watched and took care of the kids. She was always sick so they gave her extra attention, not knowing how serious this was (my aunt hated it). She hated she didn't get the attention that she was seeking (at least not from home), older boys and men gave her attention which landed her in trouble repeatedly. It even earned my auntie a few beatings. She was a beautiful young lady just lacking confidence. She was slim and wanted to gain weight to become thick, but when she got thick she wanted to lose weight. She was never satisfied with herself and became sad, placing herself in competition with every woman in sight, mainly me. I thought she was fine the way she was but she just needed to build up her self-esteem. "Some called her evil, I called her Satan's Queen. You may wonder why I thought such a thing, you may say man, that's mean, but you have no idea, the things that this Queen was capable of. How could a person have so much hate in their heart and love to see another person hurting? They smile, they laugh and enjoy seeing others pain and demise. Do you remember that saying, misery loves company? How could you delight yourself in evil? Why not just be nice and bring peace, joy, and happiness. It is no one else's fault that you cannot enjoy the good things in life. We all love you but you allow the enemy to play in your mind, he makes you believe that everyone is against you, but that's not true, we love you, we want to see you happy, living the dream in the fullness of God. Smiling, joy in life having peace truelove and happiness "real happiness" that does not come from things but peace that withstands all, and surpasses all understanding. We want you to have all the promises of God. But it requires obedience, sacrifice and loving one's self. It doesn't take much, not much at all to receive the blessings of God. I see a change in you, you look different not just in appearance. The Lord has softened your heart, from a stony heart to a heart of flesh, you can feel now, you have emotions that are not all filled with hurt, bitterness, envy, hatred and lust and now he's dealing with your anger, you're trying you smile more - starting to love yourself and love your children thinking of others. You being a mother, controlling your anger, even trying to be nice, but there is ole slew foot, whispering in your ear, the world is against you, so you become defensive, because of your fear.

    The Lord says: "my dear have no fear but trust in me, I will fight your battles you just wait and see that I am God. The creator of all things, without me nothing was made, I'm your protector, comforter, sword and shield, the creator of the heaven's, who had also spoke to the storm saying "peace be still and calm the waters" rise the sun, walked the earth and by me battles are won, so what are you afraid of ? Why do you run from me? I just want to meet your very heart's desire. All I ask is for your obedience, see if you do this one thing for me I will grant your life in eternity and while here on earth I will do whatever you ask of me. I am the Alpha and Omega, I knew you before you were conceived, I know what's best for you, so if you ask and do not receive it's because either it was something that could have brought great harm or something you could not have handle in this season or from a lack of obedience. But you, yes you, you may be thinking to yourself, well maybe "I can do it myself" so you try and try and do not see any fruits, you do everything that is possible, and fail and cry. Come back to your first love and yet asking me for help, you pray and you plea but one thing you forget and that's me. What about my instructions what about my will; is it all about you? Where's your patience, you just can't keep still, crying to me, Lord are you real, can you hear me? "I heard every cry , I've seen every tear, my dear come back to me, your first love, have faith, patience, endure long-suffering, be humble, kind and meek, have self-control in the end I will bless you, don't grow weary in your good doing, with the same measure you give, it shall be given to you. "Good measure press down shaking together running over", be a giver, give with a joyful heart and watch me work sincerely" The Lord…"

It was fifth grade, at the Mary McCloud Bethune elementary school cheerleading team competition and I remember it like it was yesterday. My mother went with me to support me as I competed against other schools. She didn't have a car, but we still spent a lot of time together, at carnivals or anywhere that you can picture that had a bus route; we were there. She had the sweetest heart, not just to me, but to everyone. She was sick, she had kidney failure and had to be on dialysis, which was a treatment to release the waste from the kidneys, like urine. The process contained two bags with one to drain the water out of her and one to put the water back in as in if she had kidneys to release the toxic fluids from the body. As a person that would regularly use the bathroom, my mother was unable to, and she was always in and out of the hospital from infections and from seizures. It scared the heavens out of me because we could have been anywhere doing anything and she would just fall out and start shaking. It was as if she was dying and I didn't know what to do. I also remember her talking to me often about a lot of things, but not everything because I didn't know she was dying and I guess she knew that one day she wouldn't be around. One day she told me that when she was pregnant, the doctors told her to have an abortion because there could be complications and I would have come out blind, and she could die while giving birth or immediately after. She prayed and she praised the Lord and decided to take that chance. She told me she trusted God and she lived until I was twelve. That's when she passed, I was in denial and devastated at the same time and immediately tears ran down my face.

"Crystal, Crystal, wake up are you alright " I zoned out, meanwhile back at the school I reached out to grab my cousin and told her that her favorite aunt just died. She started to scream "No!!" and I held on to her as tight as I could. A couple of days later was the funeral, which I was cool up until the day of. We got all dressed up in our red and white; I had on a white dress with red accessories.

I never got to view the body and I didn't want to, so I didn't know what to expect. Why was this day playing over and over?

We arrived at the funeral home and had seen people we hadn't seen in years. It seemed like everyone we knew and even people we didn't, showed up. The funeral started and I was still fine until they made our family move closer to the body. Returning from the bathroom back to my seat, I pictured it as my mother being a person foreign to me until they placed me in the first row. I began to rock and shake staring at her lifeless body. She looked so cold and I cried in disbelief because my mom, the woman that raised me wasn't moving anymore- the woman I became close to over the years. The caring, loving, compassionate, kind, hard-working provider, spiritual woman. My best friend and life-loving lady was laying still in her casket. My mom was gone forever. I cried and cried so loud that the whole block of Madison could hear me and no one inside could even hear the service so they pulled me out and took me to the bathroom. I don't remember their faces because I left my body for a moment and unable to quiet down, I became broken. Hate started to form in my heart and I began to hate her for leaving me. I tried to forget all the memories I had of her because I could not bear the pain. I felt lost and confused and couldn't understand how a mother's love could fade so suddenly. How could she leave me in this world without a covering and why didn't she say goodbye? I began to suffer great pain. I became a lost soul in this world at the tender age of twelve. I became a rebellious youth who felt that if you weren't my mama or God himself, then you had nothing to say to me. Nothing at all. And if you tried talking to me, at that point I wasn't trying to hear you. I received a lot of beatings for being disobedient, but what could you expect of me? My mama told me she was my mother and my father and I should listen to her and her alone. So, I did, but she was my boss and what do you do when your boss leaves. Who are you for me to answer to? In my mind NO ONE. I was my own boss and no one but God deserved my attention. I became grown, but no one else had seen it yet. My family always kept it real with me and I saw a lot to be so young that I picked up the game I saw growing up and used it to my advantage. My best advantage. I went from a respectful, spoiled brat, polite, caring, considerate, loving, humble shy little girl to a lying, thieving, disrespectful (in some ways), mean, beast, cunning. I got my way one way or another and I became an animal. Let me tell you how I got this way, though.

My mom had three brothers and one sister. Her mom and dad had five children and when I was a Shorty we all lived together. This was before her siblings started having children of their own. This was just what I'd seen in my immediate family but this was nothing compared to how big the family actually was. On my mother's father side I have over two-hundred cousins, about twenty-five aunties and twenty-Five uncles just in Chicago alone. My grandmother's side was a bit more than half, not to mention people that are married into the family. Anyways, growing up living with my immediate family, my mom was the oldest and always in charge. My granddad was a drug dealer/dope boy who served in the Army and had a serious temper problem. He was strong in discipline who would get in that tail as quick as his face could change. His wife my grandmother was a Fox and a dope cooker. Together they were like Bonnie and Clyde, the craziest two you could ever put together or like Ike and Tina. Only if you could imagine that but if you can't I will soon have a TV series showing all the details they had five children everyone except my mother had five or more children like everyone else in my family. My three uncles were so cool. The oldest was fly and handsome, he did martial arts and also moonlighted as a car thief. For a long time he was my favorite uncle who always found himself in jail. But he became a changed man, a man of God. The second oldest was smoke the girls liked him because he could dance them right out their pants he grew up reading his Bible a good kid but got corrupted along the way from shy preacher boy that fell in love hard to the following the steps he learned from his father dope boy and player, playa becoming a womanizer breaking the hearts of many. Last but not least was the youngest he was something else and we kind of shared a resemblance. He was the slickest out of all of the boys. This "jigga" with colder then Houdini could disappear out of some trouble and his player skills were through the roof. the things that he would say, and how the females would just go crazy and do whatever he told them to do ,now that was crazy and I was all ears, so I used to tell, tell and tell. Yes I did until I was blue in the face, I will get them caught up and get Beat up. Until my mom beat them up. The girls used to pay me and I would tell my uncles started saying you not supposed to tell on your uncles. The second oldest went on to follow his father's footsteps making that easy money and got away with it for some time, until he got caught up and found himself, in and out of jail ever since I could remember, but he helped my mom out with me, acting as a father figure and that's what I saw him as. Basically, the entire family was known as the bad bunch, the ones you wanted to stay far away from. My auntie was sassy like my Bigma, sexy with enough attitude for everybody but that was only half of her we will talk more about her later in the story.

My mom was a fighter, a strong woman! That gained her respect and she talked to everybody about their business if they asked or not. She didn't care that she gave them her 10 cents on every situation but people listened because she didn't let anybody run over her and she kept it real. Living with these people in the same household taught me about life without even saying a word. They prepared me for survival and how not to believe a thing I heard a "jigga" say, because they told lies to get the prize and I learned how to get them to do anything and everything I wanted them to do and I didn't have to sleep with them either just tell them what they want to hear I could've been rich for all the dreams that I sold but it worked I used to have like five boyfriends at a time and wasn't sleeping with any of them-seeing one every day of the week and the one especially with the one I liked the most; every day of the week. I used to have barbecues with two to three guys at the Bar-B-Q, one in the house, one on the front porch hanging with the family and one on the way. My family knew it, but I only did it because of the "spell binding" influence of my favorite uncle, which he had over me. They thought I was having sex but I wasn't. At least not yet.

I'M GROWN

Okay, so it was the year 1999, when my mom and my great-grandma passed. I was still devastated and trying to gather myself. I didn't talk much, I guess you can say I wanted everyone to try and read my mind. I wanted them to ask me, "hey Crystal how are you doing? How do you feel? Are you okay? Do you need to talk?" I just wanted them to help me try and make sense of everything. I needed to be comforted, but everyone acted like I was invisible. Nobody cared about how I felt and I was only a child that had just lost her mother. Take a second to think about how you would feel if you had just lost your mother at the tender age of 12 or at any point. The only person that you know would always have your back in most cases. If you ever had a relationship with your mother and if you weren't as fortunate to have had a relationship with yours, I'm very sorry. My mother could see no wrong in me and loved me unconditionally. I know she still loved me and how strong her love truly was, and on top of that I also lost my Big-ma.

    I remember sitting and thinking "where am I?" "Is this real?" All I could think about was them in that hospital looking lifeless and me crying. They were at the same hospital on the same floor at the same time. I woke up every day lying in the bed, looking around and the kids would get up and help distract me from my thoughts. I would prepare them for school, ironing their clothes, dispersing each child their clothes, doing hair and taking them to school. At this time I went to the same school 72nd and Morgan Guggenheim elementary school on the south side of Chicago. I remember one day getting out of school when my friend decided to come over. On that day we stood in front of the house on the porch, eyes closed in a deep kiss. Granny came home from work and was about 2 inches from our faces for like five minutes and just before six reached, I was being choked slammed into what seemed like by Stone Cold Steve Austin. My friend ran and hid on the side of the gate after she choke slammed me. I got up and she did it again, so I decided that next time to stay down. Unfortunately, that didn't help me. She picked me up and choke slammed me again all the way up the stairs. We stopped being friends of course after this incident because I was so embarrassed. It seemed like the whole neighborhood had seen it.

When I was in sixth grade in 1998, my auntie had her fifth baby. Of her five babies, the first one was Suga Wuga who was my momma's favorite, Tay- Tay, who was always my favorite, then it was Man-Man, Leakey and now my Monie who loved to dance. When I dropped out of school, I began to take Leakey to school for half a day and also took care of Monie throughout the day, singing to her and teaching her the ABC's. I was teaching her twinkle, twinkle, little star, patty cake, reading her books and playing with her. My aunt eventually moved and left us in the house by ourselves, but she would come and check on us every now and then. We had no clue where she was or what was she was doing all of the time and this was around summertime because I don't remember going to school or sending the kids to school. It was a long summer and most of the time we had food, but when we didn't, we stole the fake money in the safe to buy food or sold drugs to the neighborhood crack heads. We had a huge glass door that was locked from both sides and we were locked in the house so we would jump out of the 1st floor back porch window and to get back in we use to push over and climb on the garbage can. Thank God we never had a fire. Well a fire that killed use did have one night we was sleep we had the stove on to warm the house and pots was in the oven and they burnt handles and all this particular day everyone was home adults as well.

When we were caught outside we got a whooping one day I got one outside with a long orange extension cord. The neighbors saw it all happen, I believe that it was my boyfriend's foster mother who called someone. Not long after that, the DCFS came over and asked me if she beat me with the long orange extension cord and I explained to them what happened and how much pain I was in. After that, they took me away for a while and I moved in with my great-aunt, who also happened to be the pastor of our church. The rest of the summer I got to spend going to summer camp with my cousin "T" (who worked at the summer camp) and my cousin Danny as well. We spent time together learning how to swim and I thought they would help but that didn't work out too well. I panicked in the water Danny told me, "relax I can hold you up in the water", but I was afraid because she was smaller than me. I went back to the shore and two boys grabbed me by hands and feet and threw me in the water. I was drowning because I didn't know I could stand up so T and Danny had to find me in the water. It was close to the end of summer when I had to go back home to my auntie's house. My boyfriend came over to see me and told me he was moving to California. We hugged and kissed and when I looked up, my granny was pulling up from work. Remembering what happened last time, we ran upstairs to the back door but the back door was locked and nailed shut. Yes, nailed SHUT. I laughed in disbelief, like "you got to be kidding me." I quickly thought to hide him, but granny was coming so fast that the only possible way out was to jump out of the second-story window. I asked him like "baby, baby, please jump" and he had to or I would have been in a lot of trouble. After one last kiss, he jumped out and by this time Granny was upstairs looking for him. I told her nobody was there so she hit me and asked me again "where is the boy?" I said "what boy?" and she struck me again. My little cousin had told her a boy was here, but when she came upstairs, I had the appearance of someone washing the dishes, though there were none in the sink.

Not long after, we moved in with my aunt's boyfriend. He had this mini mansion with four bedrooms, one and a half bath front stairs leading to the front door and a half bath front room dining room back stairs. Located in the kitchen next to it was an enclosed back porch with a basement across from it. There was a back door in the den and a side door in the basement. In a short amount of time we went from being free to supervise all the time and from 54 and artesian off Western.

In the year 2000, Monie turned two and she was a little cutie I tell you. I started going to a school behind Roberson High School that I can't remember the name of, because I wasn't there for long and when I missed the school bus I had to go to the Mexican school right across the street. One night my aunt's boyfriend's brother came to visit and he was cute and I had a crush on him. Everyone was asleep except us so he asked me to come and talk to him at the dining room table. I obliged then he asked me to come here, and by here, I mean close enough to stand in between his legs. He put me on his lap asking me to tell Santa what I wanted for Christmas. I laughed and said "are you serious?" He placed me on the edge of the table to admire my body and then he kissed me and started taking off my clothes. I was only twelve and he was "Eighteen" but he grabbed my hand to lead me to the den anyways and place me on the couch kissing and groping until penetration took place. I was a virgin but to him I had the body of a Twenty-one-year-old so he treated me like one. Months later I saw him again and he wanted me, but by this time I found out that I was pregnant. My aunt told me she wanted me to pee on this stick because I hadn't been asking for sanitary napkins for a while. I don't know why, so I peed on the stick, but my aunt also took a test. She told me that my test was negative and asked me what I would do if I were pregnant. I told her I was a child and didn't know what I would do with a child. There could be no way I could keep it. At the end of this conversation she told me I was pregnant and that she switched the tests and the one she took was negative and that mine was positive. I walked out of her room in shock and in disbelief, crying inside and out, not knowing what to do. Before he penetrated me he promised that I wouldn't get pregnant; he told me that he knew what he was doing and I put my trust in him. Now I hated him because he lied to me. Why would he lie to me? I then found out he tried to talk to my cousin and sleep with her as well, he was twenty-one and married with children. I didn't want anything to do with him at that point and told my auntie had transpired and I guess she told her boyfriend.

    Everything I remember after this became a nightmare. One day when no one was home but me, I took a shower and when I got out I looked in the mirror at myself, asking myself why things were like this and dried myself off. I wrapped my towel around me and went into my bedroom and in that same moment I realized I wasn't home alone. Whoever it was came in the room behind me. I turned around, startled, and wearing a wife beater and boxers, it was my aunt's boyfriend. He came close to me, pressing his body up against mine. I asked him what he was doing and told him to stop and get off of me. He said "you know you want this" and I kept telling him I didn't. He laid on top of me holding my right arm down on the bed. I tried pushing him off with my left, but I got tired and just started to cry and lay there until he was done with me. He pulled himself through his boxers and entered me and at that moment I felt like nothing. I lost confidence and self-worth. I felt like my words meant nothing because I asked him to stop and he didn't. I lost the essence of ME. I got dressed and went for a walk and met a guy across the park and told him everything because I didn't know anyone I could talk about what occurred. I didn't think my aunt would believe me so telling her about it was out of the question. I wanted to tell the police, but who could I really trust? Who would even believe my story? I felt ashamed, so I tried to keep it all inside and it ate me alive.

    My thoughts daily were "Is it my fault" and "What did I do?" I tried to push it out of my mind like I did the death of my mother, but I saw him all the time and he would give me nasty looks and smile with lust in his eyes. I didn't want to be around him anymore, so one day when I was around my bff/uncle baby momma, Lady T, her auntie, I opened up. I told her what happened and asked her what I should do. She told me to tell my uncles and I did just that. I also told the police and my auntie got mad and said I was lying when the information surfaced. She asked me if I wasn't lying then why I didn't just tell her after I was raped. "When I asked if he touched you, you said no." I couldn't tell her because it was obvious she valued him over me, and all of her other children. DCFS got back involved in her life and she told them to get me out of her house. She told them to take me because she no longer wanted me in her house. Before she allowed me to leave, she took me to get an abortion, but before they could finish the procedure, she took me out of the clinic so she could keep the money for herself. Her boyfriend's brother gave her the money, so it wasn't like it came out of her pocket. She was just a money hungry woman. They say that money is the root of all evil and she was living proof of that. She realized though that she wouldn't have a baby sitter anymore with me out of the house and she wasn't giving up the money that came along with me to the different family members that were taking care of me.

My uncle took me in and one day she came over and said I was ruining her life. I ran to the back porch which was enclosed and it had a ladder leading to the roof so I climbed onto the roof but didn't think to pull the ladder up. She came up on the roof and tried to choke me, hitting me in the head with a cordless phone. She was hitting me while hanging me off the roof telling me if I didn't change my story and tell her exactly what she wanted me to say to them then she would kill me. So, not only was I hurting from the pregnancy She killed my baby. I think she made me kill the baby because she actually did believe it was her boyfriend's and she was trying to cover up what he did. At that point I was still affected by my mother dying. I needed her and I was being moved around to different family houses, yet they kept letting my aunt come get me because she had custody over me. I thought, "God. If there is a God, please just take me, why me? This is too much, help me lord please, nobody wants me, I have nobody." I talked to God about wanting to be with my mother and my aunt killing my baby, told her my mother told me, she was told to kill me, but she didn't, so how could I kill my baby, but she made me, I hate her, and I'm going to kill her, I'm hurting, I'm broken, and I hate my mom for leaving me lord why are you punishing me can you hear me. I miss my mom like crazy, why did this happen to me why not somebody else. After all the drama died down and things were close to normal, DCFS told my aunt that her boyfriend was not to be around me or her kids or we would be taken we moved into another place in 66 and Rhodes. I got enrolled back in school and I barely made it to graduation, still being a mother with no kids. My uncle Peewee was born from an addict, he was token after his birth for having drugs in his system and my aunt got him like she was going to take care of him but if she wouldn't have, he would have to go into the system. So, I guess it was cool, another kid added to my camp. I was staying up trying to find ways to calm his withdraws from rocking him to holding him and patting him and putting him in the rocker.

I changed him and talked to him and played with him, I sang and fed him. At 1st nothing worked, but he liked a bath a warm bottle and to be dry and rocked a certain way until he fell asleep just as all the kids but just a little harder to please due to him fighting the urge of his addiction. This was a tough test for me before graduation. I finally found a way to keep him content using a routine he got used to. He was cool, but in my mind, I was upset because I raised all of these kids, but couldn't get to keep my own. Another thing that was upsetting was my aunt was a beautician yet didn't do my hair for graduation. My hair looked like I stuck my finger in an outlet! Regardless, I always made the best with what I had. I created my own style that I liked no matter what. Everyone else said I was different, but don't hate me because I like different things then you I'm not like you everyone is different and we like different things, colors, movies, music.

May 11, 2000 was one of my worst birthdays and one of the worst days of my life. It was Mother's Day as well as my birthday so you can imagine how I felt. Just take a second to put yourself in my shoes. Spending your first Mother's Day without your mother on your birthday. Nobody sang happy birthday to me, no party, no gifts and it was a day of just hurt and pain covered by sad memories. There were no feelings, no love returned and it seemed like everyone forgot about me. At the funeral, everyone said if I needed them, then just give them a call. They told me they would help me, but it was all lies. It's the least they could do for TC. Right! But anyway, six weeks away from graduation which of course she could not be present at, was just the beginning of the worst turn of my life leading to a hell. I felt like I was being tortured.

CHILDHOOD PLEASURES

Playing tag, stealing candy, being spoiled by Big-ma and Granddad and getting everything I could ever dream of. Man, was this the life. My great-grandmother had her favorites and I just so happen to be one of them and then there were those who weren't her favorite, she had a mean streak she was so mean to them and kind to me, even when I was bad except for one time. I think I was around four and I boo-booed in the corner and because I had wiped my butt with her curtains (they were expensive too) she was so mad, she told my mother to whip my butt. The curtains weren't cheap, she had very luxurious taste, and everything that she owned looked as if she was: rich, fine China, Crystal pieces, expensive living room, and dining room furniture from Rossi Brothers, look that up and you will see why she didn't like people in our house. She had a candy store and I used to seal all the candy and get underneath the dining room table and stick the wrappers from the candy in this little compartments.

The only thing about my childhood that I wasn't too fond of was falling down the stairs multiple times on various occasions those basement stairs had it out for me. I loved to visit Big-mama and granddad they'd always baked goodies and cooked meals. Big-ma had to watch her daily shows: The Price is right, Wheel of Fortune, Jeopardy, Family Feud (which I still watch today), and In The Heat of The Night, Archie Bunker, All in the family, Days of our Lives, oh yeah Montel Williams and last but not least Oprah Winfrey show; every single day we would watch these shows. Granddad treated Big-mama like a queen. If she even thought of something she wanted, she had it before her thoughts were complete.

I remember the cold winters when it was so much snow, we couldn't drive, and we had to walk to get food, medicine or anything else. Each time my granddad got ready to go, I would grab my coat and say "wait!" I went everywhere with granddad, I told him I have to go to make sure you come back safe. I had to be no more than five years old. I was something else, but he waited and I walked and talked to him, all while thinking in my head I can't wait till we make it back home. I would count the blocks, but then again back at that age, I counted everything, and numbers fascinated me. A brief description of my grandparents; Big-ma and grandad had nine kids, they also shared a real love. They met in high school or childhood, they had babies when they were teenagers. He was a real man and took care of his family, all of the bills, believes in God and loves her dearly, still and haven't had another since her death. He's still here living being an example of a man, Thomas TJ Harding but Mildred called him Raphael or Ralph she loved him so much, but Big-Ma was a "G", so don't get it twisted.

 They were local jazz singers in Chicago Estée Lauda perfume, Adriana furs, if you came to visit over five minutes you better had called or you are not getting in. She didn't like unexpected guest. And you better not touch anything, nothing, and if you break a piece of China, ooh but if you was her baby like I was, me and "sexy Dexy" my little cousin, you could get away with it. My little cousin Dew use to always come over, I've always looked at them as little brother and Dews father, Sam use to do drugs heavy and he had two other kids by his ex-wife hip-hop and Nina they are mixed . He would stand up and go to sleep, or clean things that were already cleaned looking for things that wasn't there, I would get so mad because he was scaring my cousin and disrespecting himself. I was a five year old with a lot of sense. My dad was a crack head as well; a community of drug dealers and generational curse which first started out, as it takes a village to raise a child the whole neighborhood from grandparents to children to grandchildren then great-grandchildren all grew up together so we became family. "How could you get raised together to come up against each other? Fight one another, deal drugs to your brother, uncle, cousin, sister, son, just to make a dollar? You kill one another with poison then you turn around to kill yourself. They say "money is the root of all evil", you wanna be the center of attraction being flashy with the money, cars and clothes which builds up jealousy; hood rats, drama and hoes so now your brother wants to talk your life for the glitter and gold but you struggle to sleep every night."

Demons you battle, with and stories untold; do not become a product of your environment and leave here before your time. It is not that serious to try to live how rappers betray themselves, you want to be hard but struggling to make a buck. Work hard for what you want, because when you do nobody can take that from you, trust in God do things the right way. It may look hard, but is easy to start today; keep on trying once you get used to it, "your mothers will stop crying your brothers will stop dying." Love your neighbor as oneself, if you see someone in the need of help, help as you will want someone to help you or your child or your mother place yourself in their situation you will find it easy if you love the Lord our God with your whole heart. It will be so natural to do, not taking kindness for weakness but helping to build one another up. Let's kill the hatred. Stop for a second to think where it comes from "selfishness" replace selfishness with selflessness it is the enemy's plan that we will wipe one another out. How could you hate someone? When you hate you do not care, you are numb to that person, and you could care less about them and have a desire to harm them. What have they done to you? Made you feel bad! Hurt you! Have something that you want! Took something away from you! Out of all of the statements the main focuses is you, you have to deal with you and when you can learn how to do that your life will be fine. Can anyone take anything from you that's yours, you may think it is yours, he or she- is yours but God has something better let them have it.

One, two, three, four; I've hated four people, my aunt, because she didn't protect me. My ex for cheating on me, the girl he cheated with, because she knew he was mine, I thought he was mine, and the girl that he had a baby with I wanted him and her dead, another ex-wanted him dead, but God says "I will fight your battles" so I ask for forgiveness and gave it over to him. Some people had to be removed from my life even though I wasn't ready to let them to go, but it was for my best interest. Many people hated on me, family, friends, boyfriends and people who I didn't even know, because I looked different because I dress different, my boldness and because I'm outspoken. When they can't even express themselves this came with time. I didn't know how to communicate either. God placed his favor on me each and every day. All of us are given a chance to build a relationship with God. That's how favor is obtained, when you give your life back to him. It was a choice I made, the choice you can also make. As I look back over my life and I think about all the things God had done for me- is how I know that God is real! Not from what people had told me, but from life experiences. Most people that have not experienced God and true struggle, they live through other stories, but me, I have stories of my own. I've seen the works of God, if you don't believe me- you will. The word of God says, "Every knee shall bow and every tongue shall confess that

Jesus is Lord" and that simply means, he will show you and you will call on him.

LOOKING FOR LOVE AND AFFECTION FROM MEN

My freshman year in high school John Marshall I ran for homecoming, joined the cheerleading team, ditched a few classes, hung out in the art room for some reason I just wanted to draw airbrush and paint it took me to another world. The first day I met a guy named Hennessy he looked like usher to me clean and he smelled like curve. I walked past and I smiled saying to him I would get your number but I'm late he stopped me and gave it to me anyways then I see my girl Reesi who has been my friend for about ten years, we first meet in second grade. She gave me one of her old doll for Christmas and we been cool ever since. I love this girl I also ran into my girl money I met her in sixth grade, when I was talking to this boy named Chucky who her friend Val which turns out to be my cousin was talking to at the same time. So we didn't like each other because of him, but back to high school days me and 7 others girls started to ditch school and go hang out as soon as the bell would ring we would bust thru the doors like torpedoes and start running to the bus stop or hiding in stores because the security use to chase us ,we would ditch to go downtown without any money we danced sang had fun screaming laughing and acting crazy we started stealing clothes to stay fresh and we stole costumes for Halloween one time we got caught, it was funny by the way it's not cool to steal we could have gotten serious time, but they called our houses instead but we tried to run out of the store and the security got us coming up the escalator so one of our friends tried to jet back into the store and ran right into another guard we looked at the tape and it took all that was in me not to bust up laughing. Man we had some times but we all learned valuable lessons in life and we had a bond a true friendship and we are still friends today I love them all. Not long after I got kicked out of school for missing too many days because when I wasn't ditching my aunt kept me home to babysit her kids.

So I missed more days then I went, but after being kicked out I still went, but it was too late it didn't count for anything. It was better than staying at home and I didn't have anywhere else to go. All I know is that I left the house every day, well most days. I went to the mall or downtown until, I started to talk to Dre then I started going to his house. I Thought I wanted to be with him forever, but it was just too many females that knew him. Every time we went somewhere it was "hey Dre!" I use to be to so mad. He would say to me "baby I only want you, I love you, I'm not cheating, and they just know me". I think we lasted for two years or almost two years and I broke it off well he did when I told him I got married.

Trying to distract myself from pain I made myself forget some things I looked for friends to feel the void started hanging out with females going to juke parties, being fast liking boys and all the boys wanted to do was have sex. I thought maybe one would love me. I went from knowing the game to falling for it, because I wanted to feel loved. All I was doing was being used letting them tell me we was gone be together, tell me that they loved me, tell me that they want me, then cheat on me. I would find myself laying underneath them crying inside asking myself. Why? How? Not again, I just wanted to get out of there feeling used, stupid, lost, and confused. Thinking how I end up in the same position over again letting guys have their way with me. When I don't even like sex, a few times I thought I was in love, but I like the way they treated me, or how they look. Oh let's not forget swag, all and which are not good reasons to fall in love, or to think I was in love. Some of the guys were grown men, a bus driver, and a police-officer, guys that were my age or wanna be thugs. It was a journey getting to this point it all started with a seed that was planted, which was rape.

RAPE

This chapter is about rape "I WANNA TOUCH THE SUBJECT OF RAPE IN DIFFERENT FORMS" children being raped by family members and neighborhood friends being hurt by the ones they trust. I want to talk about this because I keep hearing stories about small children getting raped. A little girl I was babysitting got raped by her dad she was four years old. My second husband was raped by a neighborhood friend. I believe he was 8 the boy that raped him was a teenager or young adult who hit him over the head and raped him. This resulted in him later becoming gay. One of my best friend's uncle was raping her nephews. My little sister was raped by her stepdad. I was raped by my aunt's boyfriend, at 12 and at six by an older cousin that was related by marriage. A lot of incense was going on, many people don't speak on that family rape or incest. A lot of things we're told to be quiet about and to keep it a secret. Well the secret is out, it's hurting children they grow up with a complex sculpted into the individual that they didn't wanna be. Either an adult that does the same thing that was done to them to another, or afraid and gay, or they develop a sex addiction. They become products of their environment or how the world influence them by saying it's okay you can be gay ,do what you want , live how you feel, God knows your heart. Which are all words to make you feel like your wrongs are right. The world wants to see you fail but the world says, it wants to see you happy. It enslaves you, if you worked as hard for yourself and towards your dreams as you do working towards the dreams of someone else, you have all you set out to do accomplished. That's what brings happiness not stress. It's not complex, and neither will you have to deal with the disappointment of having a positive results of H.I.V or aids test, because of the lust of the flesh; had an uncle that died from aids this is real he had one sex partner that was a male for around ten years. Keep yourself it may be hard, or easier said than done, but if you watch what you listen to, because some of the music will get you in the mood. Or get you to do things, it goes through your hearing and it tells you what to do, and what you watch or see gets programmed in your mind's subconscious, latter you think it was your ideas/ thoughts so you act upon them. Let's not let a temporary feelings make a life time of trouble. Be smart keep yourself by keeping yourself you will have a better life with abstinence you can't get sidetracked or distracted by lust. You will be able to complete what you are set out to do, no matter what happened to you the Lord has brought you through whoever has hurt you in the past there unable to hurt you anymore. The Lord God will fight your battles.

    Having sex from being hurt trying to cover up and mask the issue from which the pain comes I began fighting myself I guess it was spirit vs my flesh my spirit was willing and wanted to do what was right, but my flesh struggle with seeking for something to make me feel good instead of something to heal my heart from pain and brokenness. I became lost trying to find something in sex that was never even there. I got nothing from it but a feeling and when it was over I was back filling the same way. I felt it was just a distraction for the moment. I was addict just like a crack head and I talked about them, how they didn't love themselves, or respect themselves, however I fell in the same category. How dare me, when I had the same problem, different addiction. At first I used to blame it on not having self-control, but that's where God comes in at. I had a choice to choose him over a feeling for the moment.

    I stayed promiscuous until one day I got hurt. After being raped, it seems like men began to flock to me. I guess it was the enemy at work. Some of them made me think that they was just so in love or gave a false hope that they would love me, telling me what I wanted to hear, or telling me what they thought I wanted to hear to get in between my legs. Yes I let them one reason was because I thought I was going to get raped again. I thought my no didn't mean anything, I didn't think my words had power, it was my fault that I ended up in situations alone with men. They would say, imma take you out, and take me to their houses, or motel rooms and I'll just end up laying underneath them again feeling wounded. Filling raped because I didn't want to do it, it happened so much it went from being unwilling to willing I started to make sex work for me, started to do it out of enjoyment. Just to see their faces, and watch them tap out. I became the best at what I did and it had men eaten out the palm of my hand but I did not want them it was just for fun. I started to make them cry, they told me they loved me and this time meant it. They even bag me to be with them. I eventually got tired of the life I was living. One of my aunties that was a preacher told me if I didn't change my life I would be found dead in a ditch. It shook me but it didn't quite change me well not overnight at least.

When I got married that was the game changer. I guess you can say God slowed me down. It was a process though because a year before I got married maybe, a bit over a year Rio came back, we got back together but I was still in a relationship didn't tell him about it until the guy popped up. So I broke up with the guy and hurt Rio for not being completely honest. Rio and I had been on and off since I could remember he was my first boyfriend and kiss. When he moved to Florida and I was sick laying in the driveway, wouldn't shower just sick, it lasted for months. I thought I would never see him again I was hurt and he was wilding fooling in Florida with the doors up just hitting teachers and all.

Any who my cousins and I were riding the bus, but got on the wrong bus and to my surprise who did I see a cutie, so I got out of my seat and offered him some skittles. He ignored me at this time in my life to build my confidence, I use to see how many numbers I could get in a day. I didn't actually call them I just didn't feel pretty, he gave me his number and we got off the bus. Three weeks later I called him to invite him over for thanksgiving little did I know he used to live only a block away and knew the hood.

    This year I cooked the entire thanksgiving dinner, but while I was cooking I had on a slip like towel that didn't have straps, no underwear and it was see thru. I was hot, full of lust and trying to entice this young man I didn't know he was a virgin or he would later become my husband he was cute but I didn't like him it was like putting a sheep in the cage with a lion. So by dinner time I had my ex Murphy lee over, my girl Reeci, and the family, my friend asked me if it was ok to talk to him "The guy I met on the bus" and I told her I didn't care but I got mad because I invited him. I was attracted to him but I fell back, he told me and I told him she cool if you like her talk to her but he was confused he called me on in off but I had a boyfriend which was Dre, so I was never home. I came up with a plan to get married to get away from my aunt because she took me to heart grove "crazy home" with a case that she built up against me to make them think I was crazy. She made me go back and forth to the police station saying her dude did and didn't rape me, and told them I tried to kill myself but my granny came with her and stopped her but she wanted them to grant her custody over me until I was of age twenty-five I wasn't going. I wanted to live my life, she wanted the money from the state, a babysitter, and to just make me miserable. Why? Because her guy raped me and it hurt her, "WAS THAT THE REASON WHY SHE TRIED TO GET ME LOCKED UP IN THE NUT HOUSE?" I was a child that said no, all that other stuff had nothing to do with me. She slept with my boyfriends, well some of them and hooked them up with other people to hurt me but she hurt me when she didn't protect me from her boyfriend acting like she didn't know he was raping me. So my get away was marriage, I had to get hitched. I told Dre he told me yea baby in a year, so I told the guy from the bus and he said yes we can get married he came over with me flowers for valentine's day card and bear and so I started spending time with him talked him into taking panty and bra pics of me then talked him into sex we got married I told one family member and the entire family found out. I was forced to move with him so we tried to make it work living with his nanna until we got a place of our own, but in my mind all I can think about was moving to Detroit. I told my Auntie, my dad's sister I will come back when I turned 18 she took me when I was thirteen after finding out I was raped. My aunt my mom sister reported me as a runaway, she lied to the family and said quote on quote "my sister wanted me to have her daughter she told me to get custody of her"

My papa "moms dad "told me my mother didn't even know who my aunt was. My aunt had a plan she was money hungry and money came over everyone except her man oh let me rephrase that her meal ticket. She had got an I.D. with my mom's info on it but it had her face upon it I wanted to rip her head off disrespecting my mother like that. She took all of my money my mom left me and mines savings for collage and personal not to mention the monthly checks out the bank. Mind you, never bought me a toothbrush or nothing. that really broke my heart the church my uncle or KeeKe gave me money to helped me out, and pepper my cousin my dad side gave me a lot of hand me downs thank God for her, but living with my auntie was hell and no I wasn't no angel, but she dragged me to hell.

I married my husband and moved with him then I went to Detroit to visit for some weeks came back got my things moved to Detroit with my step mom and her five kids. I wanted to try and build a relationship with my father it was the winter of 2004. I went to visit my father I didn't know it at the time but why this "ninja" pawned me off to a drug dealer, well I believe it was a good transaction. The guy was a good guy he didn't want to hurt me, he just wanted to be loved and enjoy life. Anything I wanted or thought I wanted he provided my needs and my wants and didn't even wanna have sex with me but he did want to cuddle and go out to eat and just to feel needed like every other man in America; well in the world. At least I think but any who he was nice but not my type at all. I was young, so I had a certain preference of how my man had to look and his description wasn't it. He was like 5'4, dark black, blue-black, weighed about 380 pounds but he was clean though, not sloppy, always had a nice haircut smelling good and looking good, but my type was a slim or athletic built, light skinned "red bone" mixed, looking brothers with dimples, nice smile, lips and eyes not dark unless he was "Morris Chestnut" now that brother, umm, sorry about that I got a little sidetracked back to the story. One day we went to fish express and we looking at the menu and it felt like my balance was knocked off, like the room was shaking then immediately stopped like an earthquake and then I began to levitate off of the floor gasping for air as the stars rush down from space to rescue me from earth, man, that was a ride that left me dizzy. So I had to take a seat to catch myself and gain my composure at least. I've never felt this way before about no fish or no chicken I have to

Journey

go back I told myself it had to be that cook that gave me these feelings that I can't explain but guess what? yawl didn't even know his name, but I was no fool I didn't want to get left, I didn't even know where I was and I didn't know the dude, he could've a left me at the restaurant. So I went home not paying attention to the drive just thinking about this feeling which no words can describe I told my sister and I couldn't go to sleep I felt like a pirate that found a treasure at the bottom of the sea. I can't help but share this story metaphorically. It's what he did to me, we had major chemistry but anyways the next day my sister took me to the beauty supply store and I see the restaurant so I took down the number and I called every single day until I got in touch with him, it took four days. I called giving his description and telling them the night that he worked when they told me who he was and the next day that he worked. I called him back asked him for his number saying I don't want you to get in trouble while you're at work so give me your number and I'll call you later "this is the girl who was in over the weekend with the heavyset fellow last Saturday night" and "when you looked in my eyes my heart just took a flight" we can talk about it later when you get off tonight, he said "okay" and he gave me his number told me to call him at nine, so I did what he asked and didn't waste no time. Excited, because I found him, I got off the phone screamed and I jumped up and down shaking my sister, she started shaking her head because she just couldn't understand he told me. Later on that night he knew who I was and he was checking me out as well but he didn't know how old I was, he said he thought I was fifteen or sixteen, I told him I was 18 and he told me he just turned nineteen. I didn't know his eyes were green which were my favorite color anyways all that I can say I started out with game told him where I

53

was from Chicago of course my visions my dreams and all of my fantasies I painted all kind of pictures they were vivid and I made him feel good he was so in to me we talked like this for weeks then he broke up with me because I told him I loved him he became afraid of me but in less than a week he came back to me he couldn't understand why he told me and he just couldn't stay away from me not long after he told me that he lost his job so we talked for morning every day until the night. Well next morning we fell asleep on the phone he asked me my address and told me he wanted to come get me because I was only 10 blocks away in the past we would set up dates but it never ended up that way. We sold one another dreams and hopes of meeting on seven mile when I was at my brother's crib and he was at his cousin house.

    One day he walked to my house the snow was up to his knees and if any of you know me I just don't mess with the cold and not only was it cold it was snow. but I was so gone I didn't even care, now isn't that love we walked to his house talking holding hands and by the time we reached his house my entire body was numb but I didn't even care we reached his house and cuddled under one another on the couch talking and watching TV well the TV was watching us we shared our first kiss. I was shy because I wanted everything to be so perfect. I felt like I was on stage at a talent show in front of millions of people, I didn't want to get booed off stage so I held my breath, he kissed me so passionately that it felt like I passed out and he revived me. I gasp for air and he began kissing me again my heart started to beat out of my chest skipping beats. His touch made me melt in his hands so gently, he lifted me off the couch still holding onto my hands he lend me to his room and then onto his bed and there he took off all of my clothes as I stared gazed.

Journey

And as he also removed his clothes he was still kissing me from my lips and over my body. Next, he then entered me slowly and I felt every single stroke, he made love to me looking from the window of his eyes into the soul closing our eyes and traveling into space through time with my friend, my soul mate mind body spirit and soul, we talked to one another laughed, smiled and cried, it was so powerful as we allowed our spirits to intertwine and become one changing positions becoming dizzy as we climaxed exhausted in amazement as we tried to compete for the title we both tapped out.

While lying there holding one another talking four hours neither one of us were able to move let alone stand. We first fell in love over the phone. He pulled back a bit afraid because this never happened before in his entire life. Love had rushed him like a Russian wave, we both loved one another hard and couldn't live without one another. We called one another each and every day from the time we opened our eyes. If I wasn't at his house, waking him up, being under one another until it was time for me to go home around 2 AM. Then we would talk to each other on the phone starting over at the following day. Becoming more and more with passion. Every time we would get together; not caring about nothing but one other. Being with him made me feel like nothing else in this world mattered, it made me forget all of my bad days it's like they never did exist I knew for a fact that it was true love. We would look at each other and have conversation with eyes and body language without words just energy from the universe that worked with us every time we touched, we reached galaxies.

Summer days. The air was dry from humidity, however when the wind will blow it felt so refreshing like a cold glass of water quenching the thirst. I don't know if I was dehydrated or just high, we blew on trees like Jamaica. Every day was the same thing. I'd wake up and get "fly" dressed and go outside to chill with the homies, smoke, have fun, roast each other (talking smack to each other) talk or go to the mall. Every day we had to smoke. Sometimes when we woke up in the morning we just blazed (getting high). Even though I think it's wrong now, I wouldn't trade it for the world; we had fun, but you grow from that. I remember getting so high that I would see rainbows and I had felt like I was on a roller coaster ride. It was my birthday, I was turning nineteen and at the crack of dawn we all woke up and went to Keshia house. Keshia's house was the house that everybody went to when they wanted to get drunk or high, "the party house" we used to play music and dance. You know basically, act a fool. But then again everywhere we went to kick it, was the party house. Once we broke down the blunt and opened up a bottle we believed the more the merrier and we would match each other, which means "put it all together "and be comatose. Now that I look back I can laugh, but at that moment things were so serious especially in this relationship. Like I said in the beginning, I had game, that I had learned from my uncles and I used it, but mixed it with my own twist. So a description of me was charming, an ego stroker, intelligent, street smart, a hustler, kind of thuggish with a temper, but slow to anger, I gave people more chances than they deserved. I was sweet, caring, loving but knew how to get what I wanted by all means necessary. I was shy. But knew when to speak, I was a beast/ chameleon. I could adapt to any situation and gain mind control. By just being me, made guys fall in love. I was honest to some degree and to the point, as well as a freak, so the things that I would say would "make love" to a guy's mind and they did not know what to do with themselves. On top of that my appearance from head to toe: my eyes glistened like you were looking at the sun, glossy big and bold brown eyes, cute button nose and a smile that sparkle like the stars of the south at night, medium caramel complexion, bust 40 DD waist 32, hips 36 and a booty like Judy. So I was stacked and I knew I was bad, but for a long time I tried to down play myself and cover it up because I had a lot of females that didn't like me due to jealousy because of my face and shape. By the way, which didn't really mean nothing to me. I was about love and unity, but family, friends and strangers use to feel so intimidated. Not all people, but half, I can't see why I talked to everyone, loved on people and never acted like I was too much. I've always been down to earth, people still didn't and still don't like me. Any who I'm a gaurs, whatever that means and I loved to be the center of attention. Not to just steal the shine, it happened naturally because I loved to sing and dance since I've been alive and walking. So I did me and others I guess that wanted to be the center of attention tried to attack me because they felt I was doing too much when in reality I was just having fun trying to make the best out of my situation that I was going through. I was back and forth from Chicago still trying to find myself, I was still legally married but in my mind since I only got married to get out of my previous situation of being a mom to eight kids, cooking, cleaning and going crazy, making sure homework was done , washing and ironing and taking them to and from school. I didn't have any in house siblings and was spoiled rotten. I was just used to it being me so I went from me and my mom to moving in and becoming Cinderella from the hood. Man! I hate that my mother died and the fact my aunt was just so damn evil, she tried to put me in a crazy home so she could get checks and try to keep me around babysitting longer. She tried to do any and everything that she thought would hurt me because she was hurt because her boyfriend was raping me. How did she think I felt? Because she didn't save me. My granny eventually stepped up and took me in, but the things that I had to endure before she did was a mess. My mother was in her gave doing cartwheel flips and somersaults.

    My granddad said to me "Your auntie is not right, she sit up here lied to get custody and your mother didn't even want you with her" with my aunt. She only looked out for her best interest and stepped on whoever she had to get on top or sleep with whomever. She had to distract them. My uncle said a long time ago when she first got married, she went to childcare and took the official stamp to stamp her childcare papers by sleeping with the man in the office and distracted him so she could stamp her own papers. Who would of thought? The part I couldn't get, was why she hated me so much? But any who we will get back to that. I was back and forth from Detroit to Chicago to Detroit because I was running from my family. I didn't think that none would help me to escape the devil in the flesh and every time they (police) of DCFS took me away and placed me in another home. They would let her just show up and get me. For one, she was getting money for me which I had never seen, she never even bought me hygiene items or under garments. The church my uncle went to our male friends had to get my things and DCFS. On top of that I had a urine problem; when I was little I use to pee in the bed, I couldn't hold it and sometimes at school my bladder was weak and after being raped it only got worse. So I use to pee on everything and everyone. If I peed on you or in your house I'm truly sorry like I was pissing on my boyfriends, which was so embarrassing on my ex-husband, friends, and family. That was the reason why people were like "gone ahead and take her, we don't care". I moved with so many people in my life. I lived in almost 50 different houses, that's probably why I'm a bag lady today and I'm always on the go it's just something I'm used to.

From all of this and my mother's death; I started to believe people liked me but did not necessarily care about me. It helped me to have relationships that I wasn't attached to. Like I loved, but to a certain extent. So I wouldn't get hurt from people leaving me or dying. I had that nonchalant well, I don't really care, but do kind of care attitude; like a guard up for years. I would be sad but not devastated and I always prepared for the worst with everything that I did. So I would get let down or disappointed. I was going thru all of this and had no one. Everyone had their own lives, not worried about me, I was invisible until I met buck and he fell in love, we fell in love and I forgot all the bad stuff.

CAUGHT UP

It was a new life I was lost and became of the world but found God while searching for myself because he lived in me all along but I had to go through the journey to find him. I loved buck so much I made him my God without even noticing it, but God noticed and made me release him, but we had a couple of moments that I want to share with you that I will never forget before we ended thing

After going back and forth to Chicago. I guess it made buck mad. He would get drunk or high to express himself to me and tears would be in his eyes. He would tell me how much he loved me and ask me not to leave. But my husband needed me, I know we wasn't really together. My husband and I, but my husband loved me and was in love with me and I started to learn what a marriage was. Buck was doing him with females and he acted like I didn't know. His grandma, mother, sister, brother, cousin's friends; everybody told me what he was doing. He was serious, but he was in love. He didn't know how to be faithful, but he tried. He was just afraid of what other people would say because I was married and he told everyone that I was married, he didn't wanna look stupid. I had got married to get away and it was an agreement made with me and my husband. The more we started to be around one another, my husband and I created a bond, got to know one another and I actually started to like and love him so I started to be with them both I mean neither one of them was faithful to me well at least I didn't think they was. So financially I helped them both, because I was a money magnet, money just came to me and I was a hustler so I flipped it and if they needed something I was there.

I grew up with hustlers all around me, crack heads, which are my great uncles and friends and dope boys. My uncle lived with me and as a shorty I was forced to push weight when we didn't have food at age twelve. So I thought I was a thug out here getting money but God kept sending people to me to give me a word, to hug me or

Journey

I would read the bible and get a word He was slowly but surely changing me I couldn't see it yet. My husband use to pray for me and with me and when he would play the piano. I would cry, sing, and praise. He had such a powerful anointing, but not when he started playing, it took a while. All he wanted to learn was classical music. Don't get lost, I'm not jumping around I'm telling you the story in order and let me remind you this is only the 1st book but anyways, back to the story. I was in and out of Chicago sometimes for months at a time.

One day I was in Chicago, at evergreen plaza on 95th and Western, strolling through the mall window shopping and wound up in this urban clothing store in the basement looking around and an attractive brother who looks to be about twice my age came down to see if he could help me, he looked me up and down and I said to him no I was just looking. He then asks me for my number and I gave it to him while he entered it in his phone. A few days later he called and started to call on the regular until he got to take me out at this time I was going to massage school so I took one of my classmates with and he invited a friend of his. However the date wasn't really a date they drove us into the middle of nowhere we had no idea where we was. They drove us to a motel when we were supposed to be going out to eat, we were like what the hell is going on this for sure don't look like no eatery, but we played along not wanting to upset the guys not fully knowing them or what they were capable of doing, we just went along with it because we didn't have cell phones and we did wanna make it out alive. I was feeling this cat, but not enough to give up my goods, but I thought ok a one night stand won't hurt it will all be over soon and it was they took us back

Journey

to the city and dropped us off when we learned a lesson not to trust people who you don't know and always have a way of letting others your location keep a phone and it's better to meet your date at public places.

    I went back to Detroit for a couple of months and came back to Chicago to visit and to my surprise, this man was posted up outside waiting to attack like a vulture seeking its prey. As I walked up to the door and placed the key in the first lock I didn't have a chance to attempt at the other three. I was being ambushed. I never even seen this man come up behind me until he spoke "get in the car, why haven't you returned my calls" he said angrily and agitated. So I quickly responded, I didn't know you called I was in Detroit, I moved after I last had seen you; he said, oh so that's why I haven't seen you, which led me to believe that this wasn't his first visit. Stalking the house, I tried to remain cool and act normal, "so how you been?" but it only made things worse, he didn't really wanna talk he wanted me and his mission was to get me. I can't remember word for word that proceeded out of his mouth after, because everything became a blur. I knew I was in trouble and it was nothing that I could do it was only three houses on the little street we lived on. My granny and her husband were knocked out they wouldn't hear me if I screamed. So now what I needed was a plan that would work, because if I failed at it, it could end in my death.   So   I didn't want to upset him so I acted as though I missed him, gave him a hug while I sat across him in the passenger seat. He placed his hand between my thighs and tried to play with me, I said, baby I can't it's my lady time, he didn't care, just became more aggressive and I didn't know if he thought I was lying or not because after my statement he began to climb over on me with one hand. He then, ripped my panties and with the other hand choked me to the point of me shaking, because I couldn't breathe, even gasp for air just tears rushing down my face. So when he had reached the point of his climax and was finished with me and then he had let me go. It never felt so good to breathe again, I got out of his car and went into the house sobbing and unable to find my tampon. By the time I got in my room before I could hit the light I threw up everywhere a lot of vomit shot out like the movie Extasis, and not only was I vomiting I started to have a bowel movement just as bad, all liquids shooting from both ends unable to control it. My granny woke up to use the bathroom and heard me crying so she came in the room and start asking me if I was alright, I told her yes because I didn't want her to worry or get upset. I began to clean up the mess journal and I sent this to my uncle who was locked up. I couldn't tell anyone that was out and risk their freedom and besides, I came up with a plan to take care of buddy myself. I had to go out west to grab a glock and I was gone air (shoot) Evergreen Plaza out. All I could imagine was shooting him in his head and chest, but the Holy Spirit came in trying to calm me saying "I got this" but oh did I fight with the spirit. It was like a brawl against my flesh. I'm good, this one is mine. But a faint voice said "vengeance is mine". So I called my little cousin sugar and she was down with the mall shootout, she wanted to do it herself, she had to be no more than 15 but very protective and always had my back. After talking to Sugar I prayed and called my sister Car and she was like come home, just come back to Detroit. Coming back and nobody really knowing what happened was crazy, I smiled like normal and started smoking more and hanging with my guy and his people. Every now and then I did massages, if I didn't have the money because I couldn't find a job, but then again I was never really looking. I was just trying to make some sense of things, like why me? Why are all of these horrible things happening to me? I soon had to even stop giving massages because guys kept asking for happy endings in which I didn't even know what that was, but it sounded fishy to me and was never taught about in massage therapy school. My step mom lived in a two bed room house, was taking care of ten people three kids and seven adults in a two bedroom, until One day she snapped out "get out! Everybody has to go!" now what do I do? My guy lives with his mom, we're eighteen and she's not having it, shacking up isn't in her fortay, she's not for it. So I stayed a few nights at his cousin's house and when his brother found out about my living situation he tried to hook me up with this guy knowing I was his brothers girl. He didn't care he needed this connect and I needed a place to stay so everything started out cool we double dated, him and my sister, me and pimp daddy Cain that wasn't his name but how he looked. It could've been everyone in the "D" knew this cat, but anyways red lobster, starters, and the side shacks were slick which means, good he thought I was his girl until he tried to touch me and I was like oh boy, I'm his brother girl. After that they found out that they was cousins he wasn't mad he was a player about the situation he still blew his "ganze and purp " pineapple Kush with us and hung out my dad thought he was my pimp because of his drop top caddy n pressed out hair but he was a smooth player and we still cool.

    I checked on him from time to time. I use to ask him for advice. Buck did as well, he was sort of like our counselor so to speak, and he always looked out and tried to keep us informed. When I didn't have a place to live he allowed me to move in the after hour. He also suggested that I move into his house but I think that would've been inappropriate because I was his little cousin girl but I guess they knew what Buck was doing when I wasn't around. Everybody use to say you can do better why him? Or he's a whore. This came from his family and his brother tried to take me on a number of occasions. Asked me to move away and have his babies but I just couldn't do that, I looked at him as my real brother and I thought it was bogus to his brother unless Buck didn't tell nobody how he really felt because he never really showed it unless he got drunk, that's when he would get all in his feelings. I got tired of the little games he played when I was pregnant laying at his house in the bed he had another chick miss piggy braiding his hair. His ex at that, I snapped out and was about to tear a hole in that chick. She was invited to the barbecue by his sister, she loved excitement and a good show. So we gave them what they wanted a show, I was ready I went and sat on his lap outside and she was pissed, females be tripping I swear, but any who. This wasn't what she wanted I told her to meet me at the store so we wouldn't be disrespecting his mother's house and she talked crap from a distance. Not long after I lost the baby, I remember when he learned I was pregnant we talked about a life together, moving into our own and stacking money holding hands going for walks looking at the stars. We spent a lot of time alone, but I wouldn't talk. I became shy or more like stupid around him unless I was mad. I had to get upset to express myself and still sometimes after that I still didn't talk I texted him or wrote him letters love letters and sent them in the mail. He was my world, being with him I lived in a fantasy world which helped me to escape the pain I experienced from my reality. I was homeless, felt alone, nobody to talk to, family jealousy and I couldn't be myself. I was so charismatic I would sing, dance, hug and drew people in with love;

loving on them, and would just engage them. And don't let me dress up, because I was already attractive it just added fuel to the fire. People would think I think that I was too much, but I was cool and down to earth very giving and kind with a smile to light up a room. But still had haters so I tried to cover up my beauty when I was around people with low self-esteem or lack of confidence because I wanted them to like me. I was a people pleaser, even Buck would get jealous sometimes if I went harder than him, but most times he was supportive that's until he became distracted by females. He started doing him so I started doing me. That is when I met Ralph a rough rider from the eastside of Detroit. He was crazy, a thug, hothead, but a fine Dominican, Redbone, milky smooth skin, muscular built, 5'6, bright white teeth, perfect smile, curly hair, and dimples, freaky and blessed if you know what I'm saying. We took a lot of showers together and had fun, I never wanted to go back home. Smoke and stroke, at this time I forgot all about Buck and he wasn't worried about me until he seen Ralphy, he took a double look. Ralph ended up going to jail. So, I and Buck got back down, but I had to go back to Chicago for a second. Four-thousand dollars in babysitting checks showed up in my name and so I had to go get that ASAP!

Me still trusting people I went to use the bathroom of a guy that worked at the YMCA because he was dropping me off at home and since we was passing his house in the process he said he had to make a stop.

Little did I know, he was crazy and he had an ulterior motive after coming out of the bathroom? I looked around for him, unable to find him I realized I was locked in his house and I needed a key to get out. I was on the third floor of his apartment building with bars on the window, and doors, there was no way out; you needed a key to get in and out. There was no cell phone just to leave me wondering how I was going to escape. Hours later he returned, I asked him where you have been. He replied, "Had to run some errands", so I said oh okay acting as though things were okay because I didn't want to upset him. He grabbed me, started hugging and kissing me and began gracing my shoulder rubbing his hand down my arm, then grabbing my hand, leading me into his bedroom, although I wanted to pull away, I was afraid that if I did, he would have hit me so I acted like he was my boyfriend or someone I liked or had an interest in.

    While over and over, the rape played in my head, as I cried inside just wanting for it to be over and when it was, I laid in his bed not wanting to move. Afterwards, he got up and left the apartment building; went on for a week until he let me go. We never even held a conversation, he just did what he wanted to do to me. So one day when he left I got up and started to look through his things, to at least find out his real name to report him. I grabbed a letter with his name on it and put it in my pocket. I was so happy to be free that I forgot I even had the letter. This situation made me stop trusting people. You would think I would've already come to this conclusion, but I gave people the benefit of doubt, gave them trust without them earning it. I looked at everyone as they had the same heart as I did. I just allowed me to let myself down, time and time again. To me it seemed like everything just kept repeating itself like déjà vu, but it was just me reenacting the situations that I put myself in until I learned the lesson. I felt like Alice and wonderland, falling into a hole to crazy land and didn't know how to get out. I became lost and confused, and to gain understanding I started to cry out and ask God why me? Why do people wanna hurt and do things to me? Not really knowing that I had control over that before I got raped at 12. I felt so grounded, confident and like I could conquer the world, but when I said no and he took it, I lost myself. I felt like, I didn't mean anything to me, dirty, and invisible like I didn't matter, like my words meant nothing. Being raped, took not only my most precious possession, it took everything away that made me; and it changed the course of my life. I was giving up slowly but surely my fight and determination were gone, I needed my energy back. I needed someone to believe in me, someone to love me the way my mom loved me, I looked for it but couldn't find it. People have been faking it, the love was conditional, because they wanted something from me at the moment. I felt that I had nothing else to give, I was hurting badly and I just couldn't admit it, I smiled outside and cried so badly inside. I felt deserted like an abandoned building, a school with different rooms and doors that was locked with gifts stolen away. I didn't know what to do so I distracted myself in relationships, well what I thought was relationships, but it was guys using me to sleep with me and keep on moving. This went on for a while until I had realized what was going on, don't get me wrong, I knew the game but I became blinded because I wanted to just be loved; a love that they could never be able to give. Eventually I found that love of God, but before I did, I started to have sex to make me feel loved, to fill the void. I self-medicated myself with an addiction of becoming a sex addict getting a thrill out of it. The way I could get on top or throw it back and make them moan and say things like "I love you" until they started to believe it. I went from not liking sex to becoming a master at it, making guys go crazy not orally, but I used miss kitty to control them, but all I wanted them to do was go to church and get their lives together. I don't know why, but I always had a desire to push people to be the best and do right, even if at the time I wasn't, which was strange, I have seen potential in everyone, but most of them didn't believe in themselves and ended up letting the dreams for their lives fall by the waste side.

While I was doing all of this, I was still married most of it happened before I had got married and when I got married I kind of slowed down. At this time I was only in Chicago because my husband called me to cash the 4 checks that equaled to like 4000 dollars, you might be reading this and shaking your head saying wow she was married but to me it was an arranged marriage to get out of the situations I was in. As I stated before, I did learn in the process of being married for almost 8 years how to be a woman and a wife, although we were separated for most of our marriage, we still was best friends, kept in contact, praying, talking, and giving advice and or financial help. I thank God for him, he helped and saved me from destroying myself, he loved me how he wanted to be loved. We both were going through, and just wanted to both be loved, but I couldn't see it because I was blinded by what I wanted. All the hurt and pain, if it wasn't someone or something that would bring hurt or pain it seemed like I just wasn't interested, my husband was a good man, gave me flowers, cards, and just wanted to spend time; ok he looked at females walking, signs, every now and then and by female walking signs, "he would say I was looking at the billboard or sign" if a female walked by and he wanted to play it off so I wouldn't snap because I was a bit looney like the looney tunes.

So I cashed the checks and made sure my husband was cool on hygiene, food, clothes and a few wants because I felt obligated because he was my husband and he always looked out for me. I also did some shopping for my boyfriend back in Detroit, at this time I was having sex with both of them I went back to Detroit. My husband and boyfriend told me they was burning after they had sex with me, but my husband was in a relationship and my boyfriend, who knows what he was really doing. His family told me females were always around, so I'm thinking like it wasn't from me. I got it from one of them and passed it to the other one then I found this paper that I had in my pocket from the man's house that I took but never reported him the paper also stated he had chlamydia and gonorrhea. So I did give it to my boyfriend and husband because my kidnapper gave it to me, we all went to get pills and a shot but it had them upset with me. I never told them about me being locked up in a man's house and being kidnaped. Not only because it sounded stupid and made up, but because I just wanted to forget it.

So now that I touch down and was back in Detroit, so happy to be back in the land of the free. I called it the land of the free because I didn't have people breathing down my neck trying to tell me what to do. I made the rules for my life, nobody tried to control me and make me watch the kids, and I just made me.

Riding with my boo Buc to drop his cousin off at work, just cruising listening to his CD because he was a rapper that made beats and some other tracks he put together. Bobbin my head feeling his beats we arrived at da ja vu , so I asked what is deja vu he answered a strip club.so I was like oh ok and as we pulled off thoughts of the club stayed on my mind I wanted to go in but I thought it was wired so I didn't ask.

Journey

My guy and I would kick it daily smoking, talking running errands and just chilling we loved making each other smile playing wrestling until we ended up kissing and no need to say more you can bout imagine we couldn't keep our hands off each other. He uses to dig in my nose or just play too much, but I loved the attention, I just played hard to get. His phone rang, we had to pick up his cousin from work so this time I decided to go in he came by I asked the DJ about amateur night he said it was on Mondays and he explained "you dance to two songs and we see how the crowd responds to you and you get to keep the money you make so come back on Monday if you're interested and you can request a song and strip down to your undies". I was down, didn't sound too hard being that I danced to hip-hop and house music my entire life since I started to walk, I also danced and won every dance contest entered. So almost a week went by, it was Monday and show time! I went to the DJ booth and requested 50 cent disco inferno and you already know by 112 but I didn't know a thing about being sexy I just turned nineteen so I bounced, shake and danced normal while taking off my clothes and made almost six hundred bucks, not bad for ten min or less. The club has seen how well I did and offered me a job couldn't say no to that, to me it was actually fun little did I know all that came with this profession. I was placing myself in danger and I didn't even know it. I told my guy how much money I made and we both agreed this could work my stepmom wanted me and my sister to leave because her house was full to capacity, but once I started working at the club and being able to buy clothes and dance clothes and cell phones and take everyone out to eat I forgot about saving to get a place. I was a kid with money just as soon as I made it, I spent it even quicker, oh, I forgot to mention this club was a fully nude club and some days I would look into the mirrors around me, see myself and run off stage crying because this wasn't for me that's where "pineapple Cush" came in. I started to smoke and calm down, telling myself I was just at home dancing in my mirror. As time passed, I became relaxed but competitive and didn't like anybody to dance to the songs that I liked. If they requested them, I used to go crazy and dance against them on the floor and make all the money they would've made on stage. I was a beast and my body was firm and tight, definition: flat belly, no ABS, tight thighs, but not too tight, body sat up and stood at attention, perky big boobs, and I didn't work out. I was killing the game and some females wanted to hang around because I was getting money others just jealous and plotting, but I didn't care I prayed every night because I knew I was in danger making these men lust after me, but I promised God if he kept me I would stop. Some nights I was at the club ministering, a lot of guys just came to converse about their lives or to try to wife up the dancers, but by this time I had sex appeal and I was full on energy and was making between $14-16 hundred a night I couldn't stand around talking I had a show to give when we heard the siren we had to all get to the stage and they would call us out by name. However, If we wasn't able to get to the stage we got fined $20.00 I think, but anyways, I braked danced, crawled popped, shake, bounced, killed it every time; the club would go crazy clapping,

Cheering, screaming like I was Celine Deion or Michael Jackson it made me feel good started to call and ask if I was dancing that night. Sometimes I had props and my dances told stories. I pictured me and my boo having time alone. I had so much fun dancing but at times felt so uncomfortable because I knew I was hurting GOD and it was more money, more problems, people started

Journey

to use me for money even my guy. I started switching up clubs met this girl named Dangerous, she was like 250-300 pounds, but had a heart so I loved her, we became best friends we danced at Watts on ladies night and the Brass Key. I ended up stopping dancing for a while and getting a place no job and no car. Eventually, had to start back (dancing). I and my guy were on and off, he didn't really, wanna help me get to work. He started doing him (the typical male thing). So my sister or cousin started taking me and my sis use to stay with me and watched my back. The clubs started asking for dance licenses which were like $300 dollars. So one day, Buc took me to get my dance license and on this day he almost died, scared the mess out of me! I actually messed my pants (joking) but I thought I did, he almost got hit by an eighteen wheeler truck; it brushed his clothes as tears rolled down my face. I was unable to speak. I couldn't move, if he would have turned slightly, he would've got splattered all over me. To this day, he said, "I saved his life" because if I would've said "watch out or tried to stop him," he would have looked at me and not seen the truck.

  Went back to the club showed my dance license and started to work. I met this lady named Zoey the first thing I noticed about her, was her boobs they looked like "Dolly Parton" or basketballs on her chest and then she stood up and shocked me cause she was sitting on a pair as well, so I asked if I could touch them, she laughed and said "yes" to me. It was very strange, she looked like a Barbie mixed with implants. Something I'd never seen in real life before, so I touched her implants and they were hard, but; she was cute and I guess she knew rich guys and ran the club. Everyone did what she wanted, everyone, but me. I liked her, though. I just couldn't follow nobody but we became cool so I ended up moving in with her and I stopped dancing for a while unless it was an event. The dancing started to get old to me and the money didn't really hold value to me, I wasn't happy and I didn't feel safe, especially on the east side the sting, lie elegant, secret city, I didn't like 007 and when I first started, I used to dance with Sean Paul and reggae my stage name was "Jamayka" dances was 20.00 or 20.00 a song to talk. I really cleaned up, but I met this girl who was very attractive she made me attracted to women by her sex appeal she told me about some ATL clubs so I went, she got me a ticket and it was a setup she tried to hook me up with this guy that was a pimp he ran a script and I wasn't going he said "I want you to be my lady, I wanna wine and dine you, take you out and take care of you" first off I didn't like him and second, she told me he was her man she wanted me to meet telling him "I was hers" and I wasn't feeling the situation so I went to the club with them and the house full of girls he had with them and he was taking their money. They had me to bend, but they tried to make me work and pay them, I convinced them I would and my friend B.D. sent me some money western union to Decatur, GA and I walked up a hill met a stranger that asked me if I needed a ride I said nope you could be a killer but after walking which seems like forever I got in the car, of course after he convinced me he was a nice guy he took me to his house to meet his pregnant baby momma and she was cool but he introduced me as his cousin and his family went along with it which was crazy but cool I stayed with them for almost a month until I was ready to go back home. I left my dance clothes and clothes at the pimp house because I didn't wanna return and never went back, I loved it in Decatur, GA just under the circumstances, I couldn't stay I went back home to Detroit and had to move out of my place so I moved with Zoey watched her kids

Journey

While she worked at this time. God started pulling on my heart sometimes, I went to the club with Zoey and one day I met a Jamaican who was very nice he just wanted to be love feel loved by a companion he had two kids we started dating I became his nanny caring for his kids cooking, cleaning and doing laundry, going grocery shopping errands walking the dog and he paid me, and shad got me an American express and bought me a car. I guess he was trying to buy me, but I was still in love with Buc nobody could take my mind or heart away from him. I was gone when I became homeless. I moved with the Jamaican it wasn't too bad he spoiled me, I did my art, drawing and anything else I wanted to do, he supported me, he was a really good man, but I used him because I didn't find him attractive and all I wanted was Buc. I just needed a place to stay he admired me sometimes I would dance for him not how I would at the club but with clothes on. My sister use to visit a lot, but eventually I got tired of living in the middle of nowhere and moved back with my step mom and I can't see beach like I wanted so I started back going to school every semester picking something different a lot of the time I didn't take classes serious I went for years just to get the money, man I could a had degrees on degrees only if I could go back.

Journey

THE SHIFT

Me and my guy grew distant, so I moved to Chicago and started taking care of my granddad; man, was this two different lives! It was like wrapping thru a time zone. Living in Chicago I would have never done any of the things I did in Detroit. I got back with my husband, but lived with my granddad. The house was packed with crack-heads and dope boys and kids with a crazy mixture, but we were all family. I use to cook, sell plates and have Bible studies, they would've gone crazy knowing where I just came from and why I was trying to save souls. I've been playing in the devils den and now I was free. Started reading my word and making sure granddad had clean clothes and food, keep up his house, making sure everyone respected him and his house. I got into it with almost everybody. I was about to fight uncles and great uncles. I was toe to toe before they could hit me, granddad would say "don't touch her she's right" and saved me from a beating as he always did.

Being with my husband didn't last long, he moved away to Champaign to do ministry and I ran into my ex and we started sleeping together: Chuckie. When he moved away I got back with KeeKe, it seemed like every time Chuckie came around, not long after KeeKe came back into my life. Ever since I was like 11 years old KeeKe and I had a special bond, he never wanted to have sex, just lay up and chill, talk and help me out with cash. When my mom died he was a hustler off Congress and ran the little niggas in the hood. He waited until I was 21 to sleep with me and I was gone! I've always loved me a thug, but anyways people were talking, I just didn't know what they were saying and I didn't really care. I rode around with my girl Tee to go to the mall and out to eat or just listen to Lil Wayne like a cop car or R. Kelly candy. We fell in love with music. Me and she grew up together so she was like my friend's auntie we use to act like destiny's child, my mom use to be Kelly I was Beyoncé and she was LaToya I was ten, but had so much fun back then watching the box all night long until it went off at noon the next day because we didn't have cable.

  My husband was back in Chicago and came to me the pastors said, "Divorce you" and I was like what!! That just don't sound right. So I prayed and asked God to allow me to speak to the pastors. I went to sleep and met the lady pastor in the spirit realm and she has been just the same as when I met her in person and the man of God male pastor called my phone on that day. So as I started to draw near to God, he showed up more and more, but I was still straddling the fence. Before asking any questions I was ready to snap go clean off on the man, because I was upset so I said "hello" he asked for my husband and I said "you told him to divorce me, " he said, "oh no we would never" I will have my wife

  Give you a call when she gets off work. They arranged for me to get to Champaign and they told me God told them, my husband, and I would do ministry with them, I was shocked and I didn't believe that. I was ready, still dealing with flesh and I didn't wanna leave my granddad, he was my "nigga" and I had his back, but one day while visiting God spoke and said "it's time to move here" you would've thought someone screamed fire how I jumped out of my seat, while I was in conversation and ran clean out the room to the bathroom. My husband followed while everyone wondered what happened, I let him in and told him, from the look on his face, he thought I was crazy from the way I reacted, but all I could think about was granddad. So I went home and didn't say anything to granddad but granddad started to talk to me he said "go be with your husband" and I said "no!" I don't wanna leave you, and he talked about how nothing in this world would have kept him away from his wife. So I moved and began to work it out I was still in love with Buck but willing to let him go to work my marriage out no more adultery and fornication I was ready to get it right.

We moved in with the pastor and first- lady and went to church which seemed like every day I was like I love the lord and I love the church, but revival and church every day, man, I can get tired of the church you know and shouting. I'm shouting into a nap, fall out and hit the floor

Don't get me wrong, it was fun and exciting, just was a quick shift from going to church two days a week sometimes to five days a week I had to quickly adapt we became armor bearers to the pastors and they started to train us not long after maybe a year later, after sitting under them we got ordained as ministers and I was over youth and praise dance some Sundays he preached and I taught bible study sometimes it taught us to be ready at all times. Being in ministry was nice until attacks came and I had to realize how to war in spirit and not in flesh because I didn't play any games and I was about to order the rock changed my life and the way I did things it helped to calm me and being able to be so close to the man and woman of God was a blessing they was just a phone call away and they helped out in any way they could I thank God for them being in our lives in that season. Teaching us and giving us love welcoming us into their family feeding us making sure our transition was smooth. Then they helped us to find our own place and I started to do hair as a side hustle did college students' hair high school students and church member and I started babysitting get paid by the state and taking classes to start a home daycare. Everything was going well, I was finally happy with my husband. We lived in a clean neighborhood fresh air a small college town, Champaign- Champaign- Urbana, IL and I loved it. I found out I had family in town which was even better to get to know a family and build relationship: Which was awesome seeing a different side of the family doing things in a different way. Things went well for some time and I got pregnant and lost it, I started working as a teacher at the head start and I still did daycare on and off the teaching job was seasonal for the migrant workers I met some wonderful teachers and staff member whom I'm still friends with today we got to bond go out to eat go to training in Springfield for classes at Lincoln land college and I was invited to some of their houses a very friendly bunch. I worked at the school for three years and also started to help out as a bus aid I loved being around the children since I didn't have any myself.

However, it wasn't always like that, I had pregnancy problems and complications since I was 13 after having that abortion that I was forced to get. I had surgery to remove scar tissue among a ton of other problems that had me having miscarriages. I could barely cope with life. I had to act as though these things didn't affect me when it was slowly killing me. I couldn't enjoy outings because people were pregnant left and right or walking with kids and pushing babies in strollers. I just couldn't take it! I smiled and was crying like hell on the inside and people use to say do you have any kids and I would say no and they would say well you don't need any. I was so hurt and I felt like they were cursing me. How dare they said enjoy your life enjoy! With seeing and watching others kids. I was a homebody, I cooked and cleaned and relaxed at home and was cool with that. I didn't do much but took some classes each semester online, but nothing special I was ready for a family. I wanted a child more than I wanted to breathe but nobody knew my pain all of my friends started to get pregnant having kids left and right even my cousins and sisters. I was so upset and they invited me to the shower I had to laugh and play games, but all I really wanted to do was cry why not me. I became bitter some people didn't even want kids and the news showed people abandoning and killing kids they could have to give it to me at baby showers I spent most of my time crying in a bathroom or bathroom stall.

    The only person that knew what I was dealing with was my husband, he was my best friend he could talk to me about anything and I could talk to him about everything. One day he and I were on the bus and I see a little girl that looked like me and I had a fit. I tried to convince him to tackle the mom while I steal the child, he looked at me and shocked like "hell nawl", but I really wanted her, she looked just like me and he said no I'm getting off this bus so I cried screamed and hollered and when I calmed down I came up with the bright plan of going to a hospital maternity ward to just pick out a baby and steal one. He

Was not convinced well at least not convinced to take a child, but was persuaded I was coo coo. He knew how bad I hurt from not being able to hold a child it was literately driving me crazy everywhere I looked was a baby. I wanted to just stay in the house and so I did unless it was a church function, but it was pregnant ladies at church too, but at least if I cried there no one would notice why things started to turn for the worst in my marriage and I didn't even seem to notice. I was now a faithful woman that learned to love her husband. I made sure our house stayed clean. He always had a meal ready, when he was hungry, I didn't nag as much as I did I thought things was getting better. I worked and went to church, but I didn't support his gift him playing the piano, which took time away from us and little did I know another woman started to give him that attention that I wasn't, he kept going to the "studio" to play for a group but in this group he was interested in a young lady that was also interested in him. But I didn't find out until he was on his way moving out to ATL with the group I use to stay up at night until it was time for him to go to work to make sure I prepared him a lunch and wake up early so I could greet him. When he came into the door breakfast was prepared so that he would feel special, give him massages, and had his bath ran with candles all over the place rose peddles the whole nine. So I couldn't see why he was leaving, he never even had to wash himself up, but I was kind of mean and I argued a lot and wanted to basically run him, but my way was the right way most of the time. I didn't think it was this bad for him to be leaving. He moved away before I miscarried and had to undergo surgery but after he moved so did I into a house that my cousin owned. It had a Jacuzzi tub, nice hardwood floor, big spacious kitchen and three bedrooms, living room 2 garages and a garden in the back yard with watermelons, okra, spices, and greens. I loved this house, it was furnished so my furniture was in the garage and my baby room was put together, I end up turning it into a daycare because by this time I was licensed as a provider. I use to have cookouts and friends and family use to come by, my husband was still gone living in ATL.

God started giving me dreams about him sleeping with the female artist of interest. So I called and confronted him, he told me no "I didn't touch her" but when I spoke with his pastor about it he confirmed my dream and it was true. After this, I no longer wanted to be married or try to make it work I didn't look at it as him doing what I did, because it was me looking at it from my point of view we just did it at different times he got tired of my mess in the past and he been done with me. I just didn't realize it because I was ready to act right.

With us I guess the timing was always off all we need was marriage counseling, but we was both tired at this point. At the barbeque my cousin's boyfriend stopped by and brought his nephews along I couldn't stand neither one of them because I knew how they was by looking at them. Everybody left and I cleaned up took a shower, watched some TV and fell asleep.

As the summer was wrapping up, I got a call from the school that they were changing locations and needed people to set up the classrooms and clean the equipment the school moved right down the street from me like ten blocks away and I went for some refresher courses in Springfield took the job back and everything started to get back on track.

I wanted to smoke some weed so I called my cousin boyfriend nephew I forgot to mention he left his number and took some of my movies because he said that he didn't have cable, he dropped me off a bag and I got bent didn't see it as backsliding at the time but ok I went to the school and started to set up and ran into him it looked like he got hired to help around the school we flirted a bit and end up going out and falling in love until things started to get little crazy females popping up from everywhere and he was kind of controlling and he had a lot of guns I wasn't about that life and I started to think my life was in danger yes I loved him but people killed their mates all the time from jealousy and other crazy reasons I just felt the need to get away.

My husband came back and by this time a divorce had been already in process, but I let him move in my place and I moved out, still kept my clothes and food and everything in my place. I was cooking for two places and getting dressed at my place until my guy went off and said "I don't want you in that house while he's there! Get yo clothes and come on," he thought my husband and I was having sex, but we weren't so he would get so angry. I didn't want anyone to get hurt so my husband and I both plan to move away. I called different family members and told them I think he is crazy and they called me daily to make sure I'm cool. I talked about my guy about taking a break, he told me "a break are you crazy, I love you" as he punched a hole in the wall, he laughed, then cried while holding, me rubbing my face so I said or we don't have to, I love you too. What would you have done? I guess he was still dealing with the rejection he experienced from his past with his mom kicking him out and putting him on the streets as a child and having to be raised by the streets and drug dealers it had it ruff and I had his back just didn't want to upset him and I was scared because we went to pizza hut and they were closing a lady inside. Let me come in to order and she look as though she had been choked with a hanger lines where on her neck so I looked and said ma'am no disrespect but what happened to you she said her baby daddy shot her after she came from the hospital with the baby so I went to the car and told my guy and he was like oh that's nothing I shot my ex in the face before so I dropped the subject in shock and disbelief and I knew it was time to go but I had to come up with a plan wasn't no leaving him without being in a box going in the ground. So I went to work every day as normal told some of my coworkers and received a call from Buc, so I picked up confused as in why he was calling but hearing his voice made my heart just beat uncontrollably then he said "I need you, when are you coming back to Detroit" I got this girl pregnant. I couldn't breathe it felt like my body had hit the floor but I just stood unable to speak the next thing I said was do you need me to come handle that the gangster came back to the surface he said no I just want to see you so with all that was already going on and me planning to leave anyway now I had the destination. I had to find my way back to the man that I knew would always have my heart one day. I took off work took his car filled it up and went to Chicago to drop all of my things. I wanted at my grandma's house and put the things I didn't care to lose at his house and had my aunt cousins and granny come get everything else that I had in a U-Haul and the next day I had this social worker come get me take me to the greyhound and I was gone me and my guy went to take pictures that day he brought me to get a cell phone and when he came to pick me up after work. I was gone all moved out he went banging on the door and my cousins told him I was gone the place was empty I moved out I cried for months because I really did love him just didn't wanna die for or over love.

Journey

I didn't see Buc the first day I got back, but when I did, he had a smile on his face from ear to ear, so excited he gave me a hug. It was October tenth and sweetest day was just around the corner, he was drunk telling me he was sorry and how much he loved me, I don't know why, but the love I had for this man really went to hell and back, I have been homeless and placed in crazy positions just to come and be around him or to see him I've risked my life to be near him and he had no idea. I started to sell CDs and DVDs to get money and I see him almost every day and started working at the piston plant with him until things started to get out of hand seeing females that he smashed and him seeking my attention. He wanted his cake and eat it too. Every time I have seen him I thought of this woman carrying his child. I always popped up and never called, so one day I went to his house and my woman's intuition kicked in. I knew the car I parked behind, it was hers, and I have never seen it before and the kids downstairs lets me in. I went upstairs to find the door open my heart began to swell, but I couldn't take another step. I went to his bedroom door and waited for a sound because only God knows how crazy I would've went if I would have went in and he was touching her. Afraid of what I would see, I called his name I didn't wanna hurt myself so I warned him he jump out of bed and ran out the room so fast pulling down the stairs like he was saving my life I told my sister who was standing beside me to go talk to the girl while I had him out the way

He was in the hallway trying to convince me to leave with his boxers on. I was still in a state of shock waiting for an explanation because he told me he didn't want her or the baby and he just had sex with me the night before. I just couldn't get into it because I was too hurt. Why would he be lying in bed with her? Weeks went by, I

85

Journey

went to a Halloween party dressed as a sexy butterfly and he got mad and tried to cover me up. I danced and he messed up the music because he was the DJ I tried avoiding him, but it didn't work he had someone to come get me and when I didn't come he walked over to me, he wanted to do his little-drunk talk, but I didn't. I loved him but couldn't bare the pain so I left the party. And I was still seeing his family and friends, but I kind of fell back off him. I quit my job in December after going to the Christmas party and singing Alicia Keys" I'm ready I always" sung his songs in front of crowds, looking like a fool embarrassing myself because everyone knew our business, but I was a fool in love. What can I say I lived with the Jamaican for a while, driving his Mercedes Benz to the hood stunting on niggas, ha! In somebodies else ride I was whipping thru the city playing Rick Ross and Chrisette Michelle "riding to the music "this is how we do it all night" cruising on the freeway just me and my baby" just me and my boss no worries at all listening to Aston Martin music "would have come back for you I just needed time to do what I had to do, caught in this life I can't let it go whether it's right, I will never know ".

 Man, I played that song out riding down the freeway with my Buc, I used to act hard to show my cockiness, but he had me in the palm of his hands. His baby shower came so I went to the baby shower with his mom, grandma, and sister to congratulate him and her with the baby. He had a fit, he screamed Crystal! "Why are you here?" it seemed liked the music stopped because everyone was looking like they knew who I was and besides his family and friends, his sister and my sister was loving it; drama queens. Everyone looked waiting to see what to do next or what we was going do, he pulled me asking to leave, he was nervous and couldn't even be

Journey

himself in a room with the two women that he loved how awkward was that? My sister got all comfortable, ordered a drink and everything and I only went to the baby shower because I gave him, gifts for the baby, clothes and stuff I had from my last pregnancy, so why wasn't I invited to join the festivities. How rude is that? The girl looked at me in a state of shock she knew who I was because when they would argue he would call her crystal and he said my name in his sleep. So she had to feel awful, but I didn't care. To me he would always be mine. I left the baby shower just to be nice. Everybody thought I was crazy, all his family and friends here to show, well they always had a show dealing with us. It was never a dull moment we acted like strays fools.

    I don't see him for a couple of months after that at his brother's birthday party, he tried to get me to leave before she came but the blunts kept rolling and my sister knew what time it was she kept giving me Remy I started to feel myself and when she came and sat on his lap all in his face I got in my feelings so I got up and turned my back on them and start to shake my butt everybody seen him looking including her she got mad everyone laughed she acted like she didn't know it was me and maybe she didn't because every time I changed my hair I looked a bit different. He changed the song to our favorite song and so I turned around and got in their face T.I. "do that" I walked up and said the ball is in your court I just got a question for you, are you happy? Because he told me that he clearly wasn't and I was feeling my liquor. She got mad but wasn't about that life they argued and he played Lil Wayne "man f+++ theses niggas" ok you a good, but what's a goon to a goblin. The whole party got crunk they was still laughing because my thug personality seeped thru this heifer get this big "Respucia from   Norbit"

Journey

looking chick to come at me with a 1800 bottle while I wasn't looking but little did she know the crowd was mine. I have been

kicking it with his family and friends before this chic was thinking about, so they grabbed her and now she was pissed when I realized what just happened, I went downstairs, got a crowbar and was on my way to handle that but got tackled on my way up like nawl cool out. I already felt I owed her one they asked us to leave so I got in the car, but my sister was still ready to fight. It got crazy and I stopped talking to him.

After that, I wasn't feeling living with the Jamaican. He kept asking for kisses and wanted to lay up and I wasn't going and didn't wanna be bothered. So I started living out of my new car he cosigned for me a 2011 ford fusion and sometimes I stayed at my cousin Meka job she looked out and if I was at her job or one of my friend's house I fell asleep at the wheel red lights green lights you name it wasn't safe a nice looking female new car riding in the hood sleep in a running car. I'm so glad God covered me, I can only imagine the things that could have happened if I wasn't covered.

Sitting in the car one night I felt so broken and alone, I was tired of this and I didn't know what to do, I cried out to God asking for guidance and a place to stay. I never felt so hurt my family called from Chicago so I answered my uncle Thomas wasn't trying to hear nothing, I had to say he wanted me home now he didn't like that I had to live like that he begged me to just come back home, but I told him I couldn't God had to tell me it was time I told him I was here for a reason I just didn't know what it was yet.

After crying, I worshiped and God said write about your life I was like huh, I wasn't trying to hear that I wanted to know how to find a place and move in it without a job I needed a blessing he said

88

again write a book and so I said what a book have to do with me being homeless and alone he said write it and you won't have to worry about another thing I'll give you double for your pain and triple for your shame. I said now I'm cool, then I thought about it, I can't say no to my daddy what kind of fool would I be he take niggas out so my sad ok but I really wasn't feeling it

CONVICTION

I started to get planted back in church, but I didn't come alone everybody that I was kicking it within the world I brought to church with me got started to use me quickly to minister to others and he gave me visions about some of my friends to warn them from harm so I did and every time there was a service I was in it started to build my relationship back up with God.

I started to write and it felt like I relived it everything that I went thru I went thru it again by remembering it only made me hurt more but it started to heal me as well it reopened my wounds to heal them. This was hard I started smoking, drinking and having sex to mask my pain. God kept stopping me from making mistakes he started to remove me from situations and take people out of my life if he said no and I still tried to do it, he would close the door he was my parent and was on my head.

It's been two weeks since I cried out to God, I went to church, Tuesday night Bible study at word and action this guy that was in the choir with me asked me if I was still homeless he wasn't discreet at all. A lady walking by hearing and asked are you homeless I said yes looking at the guy in disbelief, why would say that out loud I thought to myself. The lady assured me she worked at a shelter and could help me get into the apartment. So we exchanged numbers and the next day I was at her job which was a shelter filling out the paperwork she told me I had to stay in the shelter. But I didn't want to, I much rather say to my car I said in less than a week I was in a new apartment the paperwork process fast and I looked at

over 200 apartments, but the first one I seen I fell in love with it was a one bedroom, huge living room and dining room, nice bedroom, bathroom and kitchen very cozy $660 are utilities included it was awesome, I will still looking for places not even knowing that I had the keys to this one the lady called and said would you like me to bring your keys I screamed and shouted and praised God really looked out

I stopped and looked at my apartment just last week I was In the car the lord said "write about your life, write a book, and tell everything, I will give you double for your pain and triple for your shame and you will never have to worry about a thing so". I stopped crying the lord, assured me that I would gain great wealth from doing as he has told me to do two weeks after my encounter with him. I was at church and a young man walked up and asked are you still homeless, another lady overheard him and told me she worked at a shelter that helps with finding places and helping you to get in by paying 1st month's rent and security deposit. So I went to the place and followed her instructions and in two weeks I had a place but that's not the good part they told me they could only help with move in cost, but I couldn't find a job my unemployment was $78 dollars every two weeks; who can live off of that? I had $200 and food stamps as well, so it kind of worked out $67 out of my $78 had to go to rent which originally is $660 a month, so this went on for 6months while I was supposed to be writing, I kept getting distracted and I kept stopping because when I started to write I started to relive the pain. But I was still grateful to be in my place.

This is the happiest moment of my life standing here marrying this man a true man of God , he's the most considering, loving, caring, kind man I know and a gentleman what more can a woman ask for. I smiled so hard my cheeks were hurting, taking picture after picture couldn't wait till it was all over. We plan the wedding ourselves, cooked the food for the reception, went to look for clothes at bridal shops and tuxedo shops together, and I even did my hair the morning of the wedding. But it still turned out fine without us having a photographer still had great pictures without us having a caterer we had enough food and it was great, without us purchasing a cake we was blessed with one and blessed with the hotel room at the motor city casino and blessed with the rental truck. I didn't have the energy to do nothing but sleep after the wedding.

It was a dream come true, the way we met it was unbelievable. September, 2011 two weeks late for classes starting at Oakland community college. I was also enrolled in CNA classes in which I couldn't miss any days or I would be dropped. Rushing to class trying not to be late, but it has been just my luck we were about to have a test, on my first day and I knew nothing. Then to the right of me was a gentleman that asked if I needed help and if so he would gladly help me. Not long after he told me that God said you'll be my wife. In disbelief, I said well God didn't tell me anything now help me with my work, please he said okay God will show you. The next week we showed up for class I found out he wasn't even in this class he was working helping a direct caring, patient that was paraplegic and he was only in the classroom to help him out by taking his notes, because he was unable to write. This week he told me we're going to be together and you will be my wife. Me ignoring him again, I went home and brought to my remembrance all that I asked him for earlier in this year and I found some letters also written to the Lord saying, I wanted to just be happy and obtain a husband and children and how I was hurt from not having a family. I was married once before but only to get out of being locked away, by my evil aunt yes it sounds like a Cinderella story.

All I can remember is me going to the clinic and it was an old lady named Ms. Blanche that the nurses told I couldn't speak to, I dressed her and I took her into the dining room to eat as she began to hum gospel songs so I began to sing the songs she was humming and then I began to cry from the brokenness in my heart. I was very sad thinking about my prayers being answered, I began to cry out to the lord and to Ms. Blanche I told her I was unhappy and I wanted a husband and children. And then she spoke to me saying I will pray for you tell me it will be okay. Me, unable to stop crying at the same time and disbelief because what she had spoken. Two weeks later I forgot all about the pain and I began to get focused on school. The guy Q said to me hello again, I can tutor you if you need me to help. By the way God said you will be my wife. I didn't believe him because it was five others that came before him, saying that God told them I was their wife as well. But then I heard a small voice saying "don't push him away" has this man been the man that I've been praying for since 2010. I wrote a letter to God describing him to a "T" and 2011 on a list of things I wanted from God. One of them is a man of God, a true man of God and on another list I wrote 60 things, this man made 58 out of the 60 so far but that's just part of it. He told me that he prayed for me as well, he also said God told him my name is Crystal and before the teacher took attendance when I walked in the room he knew it was me. On that very day I looked like a bum at the time and when the teacher, called my name he said it was confirmation but to make a long story short, I think the Lord, he allowed me to be counted out because he counted me in and now I'm blessed and highly favored. This is only part of the blessing it is a more to come you just keep reading.

We moved in together, will he move in we had Thanksgiving dinner, I cooked and I fed the neighbors the ones that didn't have food or couldn't cook. I cooked turkey, dressing, greens, macaroni, spaghetti, roast, sweet potatoes, strawberry cheesecake, and Carmel cake. Other Thanksgivings I loved to cook, but don't really like Thanksgiving. I like to cook and feed others, but I didn't feel like I had family around. Bigma and my mom no longer existed. December was big, mom's birthday and Christmas. I kind of hate Christmas every year I found myself crying, I feel lonely, lost and alone, even if it is a room full of people around. I just can't get with the holidays I thought maybe I'll feel differently when I have children of my own. But this Christmas we Had a dinner blessed friends gave gifts and I felt better.

New Year's Eve celebration 2012 we brought in the new year at my church new year's Galileo praising worshiping and enjoying elegant time, in a hotel ballroom with our church family smiling and laughing dancing and enjoying one another we had a new family. Valentine's Day we decorated the house with hearts everywhere purchase 7 gift for a raffle gave out raffle tickets to everyone that came in the door as well as a chocolate cover rose, we played games, listen to music, enjoyed ourselves I cooked homemade pizza, dirty rice jambalaya seafood pasta salad barbecue chicken wings and hot wings chocolate covered strawberry cookies candy and took a picture of every couple and singles.

St. Patrick's Day we invited friends over I cooked chicken, tuna salad with green grapes and green celery decorated a little I can't remember what else I cooked. Easter Sunday we went to church I believe we ate out. My birthday may 11 we had a party I had two sisters with birthdays in May. I bless them with gifts and all the mothers that attended were that my birthday was on Mother's Day we had cake peach cobbler, strawberry virgin daiquiris seafood pasta salad, chicken spaghetti I can't remember what else we had but we always had fun, I can't remember celebrating the holidays in a long time and actually having fun I basically hated the holidays since my mom and grandmother died great grandmother. It felt good to be a giver and to be able to pay my tithe and enjoy life before my husband came into my life.

Every birthday that I had since my 12th, well 13th birthday has been upsetting, depressing not really a celebration. I tried to act as though I was happy, but wasn't in the same thing with holidays. New Year's Eve as a child, nothing special, I try to stay up and do the countdown and when I got older it just became a blessing to see another year. Valentine's Day never really thought too much about it in school, we gave candy and cards never really got anything special from spouses. When I grew up St. Patrick's Day and Easter came and went. Mother's Day and my birthday was a horrible time. This is when I experienced the most pain from not having a mother and not being a mother. Father's day I tried to celebrate the men in

94

Journey

my life, but it was coming hard not having a father of my own. Independence Day; what's that? August! Always really enjoyed the month of August, nice summer days. My ex's birthday and cousin's birthday and just all around fun in the sun. Leo season, September has been always time to buckle down and get ready to go to school, October, my mother's birthday October 4th, ruff time at the end of the month is always Halloween you get to dress up and be anything, it brings you back to childhood, playing dress up having fun but it's kind of eerie. Outside Thanksgiving, I love to cook, but don't New Year's Eve came again and we went to William McDowell's concert nobody wanted to worship, they wanted him to do all the work when it should have been an experience. I was so upset with my husband in my life, everything seemed better surprises, gifts, massages he cooked did laundry, cleaned up, he really helped out we had fun could talk about anything and he showed he truly appreciated me made me feel so special. I was so grateful for years I looked for a man that would treat me the way he did.

But I started to get visions of him being gay sleeping with other men, we would be talking or enjoying a meal and I would see a vision as clear as a TV screen of him talking and giving oral pleasure and penetration. Not knowing why I was having these visions they became uncomfortable and I didn't know how to tell him what I seen. I tried to play it off and not act so distracted but the visors started to show more often so I just had to say something honey is it something that you wanna tell me I asked he said no so I let it go and on another occasion I asked have you ever been with a man? And I told him about the visions he said no and anything that happened in my past, I rather not talk about so I said ok and then we went to church and Pastor Langston preach on hidden things being revealed. So we went home and I asked again have you been with a man and he started to cry and tell me he was raped as a child and it leads him to the attraction of being with men, and he told me in high school he dated a guy, but he ensured me he was delivered so I said ok not really wanting to ask too many questions to make him feel like less of a man or to gross myself out. I felt uncomfortable, I just really wanted to know more so I asked him was he a top or bottom he said top, but God showed me both I asked how did it feel why did he do it and what type of males was he attracted to an he answered all of my questions and we left it alone I trusted that he had been delivered from it so I never asked again.

We moved in with his granddad because he said he no longer wanted to live in a place my exes knew where I lived so I agreed to move and we worked for apple. By this time a call center in Southfield, MI. The call center was 75 percent of gay guys 5 percent of gay females and everybody else was sleeping together well one or two percent was normal. I guess we both got hired and females flirted with him guys flirted with me and little did I know guys was also flirting with him. We worked most of the same schedules so I knew when he was at work we went to church and out together, I pretty much trusted him until coworkers started to put a bug in my ear, they said hey your husband acts differently when you're not around so I watched carefully still seeing no signs of gayness I wasn't worried we both started to make friends and some of his was gay I didn't like it so I had words with him about it.

Living with his granddad. People were always over it was the party house so that was different, but his granddad was cool and he cooked everyday man his wing was off the chain he had a big family, his granddad's wife's family lived across the street so the in-laws was always over as well. One day his uncle in-laws died and so my husband made the obituary and the family came over to the repast. They talked about the funeral being so nice, delicious from "flavor of love" TV show mom sang because the uncle was her cousin. So I listened and remembered that my ex Buc said his baby mama was also delicious cousin wow so I'm in the family of my ex baby momma. While crossing the street a car almost hit me and when I looked up it was buc baby momma looking like she seen a ghost she parked and went back to the house in disbelief came and followed me around the repast. I called Buc to let him know I seen her and he freaked out and said you're crazy, why would you do that you married him knowing he was her cousin. I was confused that just sounded so stupid as well as too much work I was a stalker but I wasn't that good. I started to see her more and more, but never ran into them both so at a barbeque I called her to the side and apologized for being a total b++++ in the past, but I also told her what did she expect if he was telling us both different stories and I had like ten years of history with the man I was willing to end her. But at this time I just wanted to make peace and I was pregnant and didn't even know it yet by the time I found out I was miscarrying it must have been the stress from the wedding that we really didn't have to have because we was already married. I lost the baby in the toilet on father's day. I took it out and went to show him I was so hurt I just wanted him to hurt until I was tired of being hurt by losing kids and this time you could tell it was a child.

So, we found a place and moved across the street from our job which was more convenient and saved gas, but not really because sometime we still drove to work we started to become distant I felt like he was hiding something so we had arguments because I started to question him and who he was having conversations with. I found it odd that he knew all of my friends, but I didn't know his and one day I came home from work and he was cooking and a female was on our couch that I've never met, home alone with him not family but he thought that was cool I snapped and she walked out never even introducing her. Like I was the one who wasn't supposed to be there I came home for my lunch break and called off, he had me bent and I didn't play, it's like he wanted to awake that other side but I don't think that's what he really wanted things between us started to change.

Not long after, he ate a weed brownie and died at work they eventually brought him back by chest compressions and mouth to mouth he rushed home with his eyes bloodshot red and tears in his eye he told me baby I'm sorry "I cheated on you with Brian". I tried to jump off the 3rd floor balcony to kill myself, I just couldn't take it anymore being with him went from being the best thing to the worst thing I tried to kill myself on ten different occasions in different ways only God could bring me back from this.

To be continued............

Fear-what do I fear? My fears are leaving this EARTH without fulfilling my purpose.

ENVY-I was envious because of all the time I wasted, I seen people stick it out and passed me up, but I stopped moving forward because I gave up on me.

Anger-I was angry because no one pushed me to be the best THAT I COULD BE AND NOONE BELIVED IN ME.

Hatred-I had hatred for people who deed me wrong people who hurt me deeply I wanted them. DEAD

Pride-I had so much pride I failed to communicate, I wanted to be seen a certain way, as being hard and not soft and never expressed how I really felt.

Hurt-I have been so hurt, shattered, broken, torn apart, cried inside daily, and to myself and night, holding it in because I didn't want anyone to know I was full of pain.

Bitterness-I was so bitter because I didn't have a mom and I wanted to become a mom, every time I seen a mother I cried, I was hurt, damage, if felt like I was going crazy, trying to hold my tears inside, smile without frowning, trying to make myself be happy, Couldn't go to baby showers, enjoy mother's day, see pregnant women or hold babies.

Jealousy-I was jealous of children with a mother, people who had children, children that had guidance, people that had someone to push them into their destiny, family for the holidays, people to take care of them, buying basic everyday needs, soap toothpastes, tooth brush, deodorant, and clothes.

Lost-not knowing who to turn to, where to go, or what to do.

Alone-seeing so many people around, but everyone had their own issues, no time for me. Not even a conversation, they walk past, and I cried out just to be noticed, just to have a conversation, no one ever asked me how you feel.

Death-denial, the devastation, hurt, learning to cope, learning to live with lost

Guilt-the only guilt that I have is not cherishing my mother while she was alive, I was a child and all I wanted to do was play, not knowing that she wouldn't be with me forever.

Confused-now what do I do, I don't have a mother, don't have a father, no guidance, no adult supervision, alone, lost, and lonely, I have to find someone, someone to fill the void.

Raped-I thought that I had rights, a choice, but I learned, my voice, my choice, does not mean a thing.

Misused-trying to find someone to love me, be there for me, have my back, take care of me, like my mother did but they had arterial motives., They didn't want me, they wanted to use me, to make them feel batter, but make me feel like trash.

Ashamed-I was ashamed of the things boys and men did to me and how they made me feel, all I wanted to do was be loved, not taken advantage of.

Lust-hunger, desire, itch, want, addiction, feeling of need.

Fornication-sex before marriage, creating soul ties, becoming one.

Adultery-having sex or sharing intimacy with anyone besides your husband or wife.

Betrayed- tricked, hurt, used

Suicidal wanting to kill yourself

Homeless-living on the streets without a home, place to place, strangers houses, bar, this was me all of it.

Extra recaps

SELF CONTROLL CONTROLLING ONES EMOTIONS ACTIONS AND BEHAVIORS URGES THAT COMES FROM THE DESIRE OF WHATS PLEASING TO THE FLESH :FLESH RESTRAIN YOURSELF DON'T DO IT BECAUSE IF FEEL GOOD ,DON'T DO IT IF YOU KNOW ITS WRONG OR BECAUSE YOUR BEING TEMPTED REMEMBER WHAT LOOKS GOOD IS NOT ALWAYS GOOD EVERYTHING THAT GLITTERS AINT GOLD

FEAR MAKES YOU BELIEVE OR FEEL YOUR ENDANGER OR THREATING

PRIDE IS A ATTUTITUDE THAT SAYS YOU CAN'T TELL ME NOTHING AND I WONT ALLOW YOU TO SEE MY TRUE FEELINGS

BITTERNESS ACHING HEART, RESENTMENT, COLDNESS DEPRESSION, HATERED, ILL FEELING, SHAME AND VIOLENCE

JEALOUSY ENVY INSECURITY RAGE RESENT BACK BITING GRUDGE

LUST APPETITE PASSION CRAVE

RAPE FORCED VIOLATION

FORNICATION SLEEP AROUND

MISUSE MISTREAT ABUSE

ASHAMED REGRET EMBARRASSED HUMILIATED

Journey

BETRAYED FORSAKE LET DOWN MISLEAD SELL OUT DUBBLE CROSS DECIEVE

HURT PAIN FROM DISCOMFORT, INJURY, SADNESS, FEELINGS

TRUSTING GOD
Fear I'm afraid of GOD what are you afraid of?

I used to be afraid of being alone, not being able to become a mommy, losing loved ones, and not being able to forgive. But now the only fear I have is not doing what I am called to do I don't want to mix up my wants and emotions with what God's will for my life is. I want the life he created me to have, the husband he set aside for me, my children who were formed before my womb my businesses that will build the kingdom of God my life that will represent Christ me standing on my foundational Scripture Matthew 633 seek ye first the kingdom of God and all his righteousness and he shall supply all your needs. Staying focused no distractions on the mark of God, not worrying about shelter or food, or the latest new whip but worrying about his children their souls by giving his love and help by building his church inspiring and encouraging uplifting pushing to reach their full potential helping them tap in to feel the love they so desperately wanted to feel: and which they seek for after man letting them know they had it all alone because it's you that lives within…..

OWNERSHIP /POSSESION

IN RELATIONSHIP WE OFTEN FEEL THAT WE OWN A PERSON EVEN IN FAMILIES THIS IS MY MOTHER FATHER AUNT COUSIN UNCLE NEPHEW NIECE WE PUT NAME ON IT BOYFRIEND GRILFRIEND AND WE BELIVE WE OWN

THEM LIKE SINCE THEY HAVE THIS ESTABLISHED RELATIONSHIP WITH US THAT IT WILL BE THIS WAY FOREVER EVEN WITH HUSBAND AND WIFE NOW ALL RELATIONSHIPS END IN ONE WAY OF ANOTHER BEING IF IT BE DEATH OR JUST SEPERATION TO EITHER START A FAMILY OF THEIR OWN , GET A DIVORCE ,BRAKE UP OR JUST BEING DISOWNED FROM THE FAMILY ,BUT WE ALL FEEL SOME KINDA WAY DUE TO THE CHANGE BECAUSE, IT ALL HAPPENDS WHEN WE LEAST EXPECT IT THEY WHERE IN OUR LIVES FOR A SEASON ,TO TEACH US A LESSON ,POUR INTO OUR LIVES ,TO TEST US ,OR TO JUST LOVE US AND HELP MOLD US ,BUT THEY WAS NOT OURS WE DIDN'T OWN THEM ,JUST A LOANER LIKE U GIVE A RENTER CAR BACK AFTER YOUR DONE RENTING OR A APARTMENT OR HOME YOU RENTED WAS NOT YOURS BUT YOU WAS ABLE TO USE AND ENJOY THEM IN SOME KIND OF WAY HERE ON EARTH AND WE HAVE TO RETURN THEM ONE DAY BUT WE SCREAM SHOUT HOOP AND HOLLER, I WANT MY, I MISS MY ,AND PLEAD WITH GOD WHY DID YOU TAKE THEM AWAY ,BUT IT WAS SIMPLY TIME, NOBODY TRULY KNOWS THE HOUR OF HOW MUCH TIME HE OR SHE HAS ON THE CLOCK ,OR IN THE RELATIONSHIP, THAT'S WHY WE ARE TO CELEBRATE AND CHARISH THOSE WHOM WE LOVE DAILY LESS ARUGING FUSSING AND FIGHTING MORE LOVING SHARING AND CARING. SO WE CAN HAVE LESS SHOULDA WOULDA COULDAS JUST FOOD FOR THOUGHT ENJOY LIFE AND ONE ANOTHER

Journey

REJECTION

CAN LEAD YOU TO DO SOME THINGS THAT YOU WOULDN'T NORMALLY DO LIKE BE WITH A PERSON SEXUALLY GET IN A GANG DO DRUGS OR HANG WITH THE WRONG CWROUD JUST TO FEEL WANTED AND EXCEPTED LOVED OR LIKE YOU BELONG LIKE HAVING A FAMILY OR SUPPOURT THAT YOU WANTED FROM YOUR PARENTS BUT FOR SOME REASON WASN'T ABLE TO GET FOR ONE REASON OR ANOTHER Rejection makes you feel lost and confused as well as hurt. As a child, you care what other people think about you. You want to be accepted. When a child hears, "No", they feel rejection, and sometimes they are often pushed away. Rejection records into the brain and it can devastate them. For life. That's why when somebody you love says something that they don't think is harmful to you, or heartless. Have you ever heard this phrase, "Sticks and stones can break your bones, but words will never heart" it's a lie, but words will make you handicapped. And they can kill you. Ask yourself, what is it that is in my past that every once in a while pop up that was a hindrance from rejection. Was it relationships that ended wrong? Family members that had problems with you? Or anything else that you could think of. Do you know what God says and his word about you? How much he loves you. How he can deliver and set you free.

SEX

ADDICTED TO THE FEELING OF SEX IT BLINDS YOU TO THE POINT THAT YOU CANT SEE STRAIGHT GIVING

Journey

YOU THE ILLUSION OF THE POTENTIAL FUTURE THEM NOT THEM AND THE PRESENT STATE .IT GIVES A FEELING OF CONNECTION AND FEELING WANTED THAT LEAVES SPIRITS TO DOMINATE CONTROLLING YOUR ACTIONS AND BODY BUT ALSO MAKES YOUR VISION IMPAIIRED ESPECIALLY IF IT WAS PASSIONATE OR GOOD SOME PEOPLE BUILD OFF THIS AND CREATE A FAIRYTAIL RELATIONSHIP AND OR SOME PEOPLE JUST SETTLE FOR LESS AND BY SETTLE I MEAN FOR SOMEONE OR SOMETHINGS THAT THEY WOULDN'T NORMALLY TAKE IN A REALATIONSHIP THEY DO BECAUSE THEY BECAME INTAMATE AND THE NORMAL JUDGEMENT GOT CLOULDY AND NOW THEY CANT SEE THE TRUTH AND LATER THEY SAY WHY MY BABY DADDY AINT THERE OR WHY HE OR SHE DON'T WANT TO BE FAITHFUL OR WHATEVER THE CASE MAY BE AFTER THEY HAVE CLEARLY SHOWN YOU SGINS BUT YOU WAS SO MEZMORISED BY THE LOVE MAKING THAT YOU JUST DIDN'T CARE IT DIDN'T MATTER AT THAT POINT BECAUSE YOU GOT WHAT YOU WANTED FOR THE MOMENT AND YOU WAS SATISFIED NOT THINKING ABOUT LONG TEARM UNTIL IT WAS TO LATE YOU THEN CREATED A MONSTER BECAUSE YOU ALLOWED A PERSON TO TREAT YOU OR DO THE THINGS TO YOU THAT YOU NORMALLY WOULDN'T HAVE AND IF YOU WOULD HAVE NEVER LAIED UP WITH HIM OR HER YOU WOULDN'T BE HERE NOW OR SIMPELLY BECAUSE YOU JUST DIDN'T WANT TO BE PATIENT AND WAIT ON THE PERSON THAT GOD HAD FOR YOU AND JUST WANTED

Journey

EVERYTHING NOW THAT WAS ME WELL THEY BOTH WAS ME THAT'S WHY I CAN SIT HERE AND TALK ABOUT IT BECAUSE I WAS THAT GIRL ALWAYS WANTING A MICROWAVE RELATIONSHIP JUST TO GET TO THE LOVE WITHOUT TIME TO BUILD AND HAVE A FOUNDATION OR TO ALLOW A PERSON TO BE YOUR FRIEND AND TRULY CARE FOR YOU BY GAINING YOUR RESPECT HOW IS THAT POSSIBLE THEY ARE GOING TO SEE YOU HOW THEY SEE EACH AND EVERY OTHER FEMALE OUT HERE AS A PIECE OF MEAT BUT WE WANT TO BE LOVED SO WE BECOME TRANSFORMED INTO THIS WORLD WE START TO LOOK LIKE IT AND BY THAT I MEAN DRESS LIKE IT WALK LIKE IT TALK LIKE IT AND OUR ACTIONS BEAGIN TO LINE UP WITH THE THINGS THE WORLD SAYS IS COOL BUT WE KNOW BETTER WE WAS RAISED BETTER THAN THAT WELL AT LEAST MOST OF US WAS I KNOW THE 80'S BABIES AND 70'S,60'S AND SO ONS WAS SO WHY DO WE ALLOW THE WORLD TO RULE OVER US WHEN WE WAS GIVEN POWER AND DOMINON OVER THE WORLD UM I DON'T GET IT LETS TAKE A STAND AND TAKE OUR LIVES BACK BECAUSE THE WORLD IS CORUPTED AND IT WANTS TO KILL US AND PUSH US TO KILL OURSELVES AND ONE ANOTHER NO GOOD THING COMES FROM US TRYING TO INMATATE THE WORLD AND IM NOT GONE ONE TIME SAY THAT ITS NOT FUN TO SIN :SIN IS THE MOST EXCITING FUN YOU CAN HAVE BUT WHILE RISKING YOUR LIFE BECAUSE WHILE IN SIN YOU ARE NOT COVERED AND THE 1ST THREE LETTERS IN FUNERAL IS FUN AND DON'T GET ME WRONG YOU CAN HAVE A

Journey

WONDERFUL TIME IN CHRIST JUST THE WAY YOU DO THINGS AND VIEW LIFE CHANGES AND YOU BECOME COVERED I KNOW IN YOUR LIFETIME YOU EITHER HEARD A CHURCH AND OR A FAMILY MEMBER SAY DON'T STRADDLE THE FENCE BE EITHER HOT OR COLD THIS MEANING WHILE IN BETWEEN YOU MAY HAVE A LEVEL OF GRACE BUT YOU JUSTY DON'T KNOW IF IT'S ENOUGH TO KEEP YOU ALIVE GRACE LEVELS CAN VERY AND FAVOR IS FOR THE OBIDENT NOBODY IS PURFECT BUT WE ALL MUST TRY TO LIVE ACORDINGLY

Rejection makes you feel lost and confused as well as hurt. As a child, you care what other people think about you. You want to be accepted. When a child hears, "No", they feel rejection, and sometimes they are often pushed away. Rejection records into the brain and it can devastate them. For life. That's why when somebody you love says something that they don't think is harmful to you, or heartless. Have you ever heard this phrase, "Sticks and stones can break your bones, but words will never heart" it's a lie, but words will make you handicapped. And they can kill you. Ask yourself, what is it that is in my past that every once in a while pop up that was a hindrance from rejection. Was it relationships that ended wrong? Family members that had problems with you? Or anything else that you could think of. Do you know what God says and his word about you? How much he loves you. How he can deliver and set you free.

Topic: crack heads Crack heads, I tell you are a trip. They can sell you the shoes on your feet. And might get you to buy them as well. My great uncle Boo boo, He would always say "oh my niece look like Whitney Houston, and, oh yeah, Haley Berry". Which you know, clearly, I don't look like. He was high. Because I'm cute, but I don't look like neither one of them. He would get so high I can see how he never overdoes. I would just sit and watch him, and my Uncle Sam nod off and then wake up singing or looking for something that was never there. I never seen people that would stand up and be able to sleep. Rubbing, scratching, and searching for invisible items would freak me out. But I got used to it. At first I hated crack head, and I didn't feel like they loved themselves, and I thought that they had some kind of contagious disease that made them do crack. I was about 5 years old and I see my dad sniff something in his nose, while I and my sisters were in a car with him. Then he started to act different. I got sick to my stomach. I couldn't watch any movies about drugs or had drugs in them. New Jack City, Crook land, Minister's Society, C4 or whatever movie that was in Chris Rock in it. If I see any movie with drugs in it, I would vomit everywhere. I didn't and still don't like movies like that now. Possibly because I lived with and around crack heads. It seemed like all the neighbors were crack heads, and they ended up at our house doing crack with our great uncles so they could get higher. By providing a place and my uncles and cousins sold and provided the drugs for them. The love of money. Killing our people. But when the money was flowing like it did, you don't see the big picture. And you wonder why the neighbors didn't like our family. We helped to kill theirs by providing the poison. And I say we because I'm guilty too. I used to ask for money, and it was dirty money. To buy candy or clothes, personal hygiene, but I did ask them to stop over and over again. I was a child, they didn't listen to me. And I still had needs. It wasn't like no one else was helping me. I didn't like it, but I accepted money, and always prayed for every one of my uncles, my dad, and all of the crack heads. A few of them came to me for prayer, and all I would say was "why? Why are you killing yourself?" and they would tell me their stories of how and why they were using. But to me it just wasn't good enough off a reason. It was like eating rat poison and drinking bleach. I thought it was stupid. But God began to soften to heart to crack heads and he told me they are people as well. And some are your family. And so I started to hug them, to cook for them, to give them gifts. And I noticed that inside the crazy appearance was a person with a heart, that made mistakes and that got caught up and lost in something like a maze. And they need me, so that I can pray .Because they can't do this by themselves. So I picked up my bible and started reading around the house. And praying as I went for walks around the neighborhood, but the devil was busy working on me as well. As I was trying to help them. And he didn't appear as the devil with hors, red face, but now that I'm older, I can see the ways that he come in.

    I would be outside playing as a child at my friend's house, or at my cousin's house, and we would play house. And playing house you need a mom and a dad. And kids of course. So, it would start off innocent, but if we didn't have a boy to play the role of a dad, another girl had to play the dad. And then we would play "getting rocks and grass to cook" or we had play food with a play stove, all the things that you remember that came in a play house kitchen. We would have our dolls that we would make the children or other kids as our children. We would end up kissing and trying to freak each other to do what we seen on TV or on our older family members doing. We would do everything we seen. Get caught, get a whooping, and just play house again on another day. Some of us had

Journey

older friends, family members, or adults (perverts) try to play with us. Which in some cases, ended in rape. I heard so many stories in which this happened.

    I went to a sleepover at my cousin's :cousin's house she had to be, maybe, three, four, years older than me, when everyone went to sleep she took some girls into the bathroom, and made us suck on her boobs and do some freaky things. And I also remember building clubhouses in the yard with sheets with neighborhood friends and cousins. We would finger each other, jack off the boys, kiss, and try to have to have sex. Saying all this aside, watch your children. Because you send them outside to play, and they playing. And you think that its innocent play, and they're doing what you do in the midnight hour. You have to watch what you do in front of your children, and you have to watch who you send them around because you could be putting them in harm's way. After a child has been touched sexually, in most cases, they pick up the instincts of a predator, and they begin to touch others. And do what was done to them.

    From spoken word in the library study room: I'm just mentioning this now because these are things that we keep silent about. We push it under the rug. And if not handled properly, the child can grow up and become crazy, and/or desensitized. Nobody acknowledged their feelings. Or vindicated the act that occurred. They become promiscuous. And/or the predator themselves. And then the cycle repeats. Most times throughout family, it plants a seed of incest. And sometimes children are born and when a child is abused, they become angry and afraid, confused, and try to reach out and find ways to tell somebody. But not sure who would believe them because some adults say "you're lying "or they use verbal abuse. And sometimes the person that committed the rape threatens the child, manipulates the child, or frightens the child so they can continue to have sex with the child. Leading the child to believe that it's the right thing to do, no one will help, or that it's their fault.

From rape brochure: So they feel guilt, depression, shame, shock, sadness, denial, They can become anti sociable, they might have nightmares, feel uncomfortable around the sex that initiated the act, experience flashbacks, and may need medical treatment, or counseling or somebody to talk to. Some people turn to drugs, alcohol, try cutting themselves, killing themselves, prostitution, promiscuity, and/or become violent.

About rape: my little sister was raped at 2 by her stepdad. And she became very violent. She did not like being around males for years, and when she got older as an adult, all of her relationships were abusive: she had to fight. She couldn't live a normal life. I remember one night she spent the night at my house, and she was out late. She came to my house saying that she stabbed a man in an alley in the head. She didn't know if he was dead or alive. I let her in the house and held her and rocked her to sleep. So it was like a traumatic flashback of what happened when she was a child. I had a friend whose uncle was raping all of the nieces and a few nephews. A few nieces ended up pregnant, some kids had disabilities from the incest. And right now to this day, the issues have never been addressed and the people are hurting because it's like no one had their backs; no one protected them. And they've had to live with this and around this predator that continued to rape them for years. Pastor Joyce Myers her father raped her for about twelve years ("I think?"). Some people are not as fortunate to make it through rape. They self-destruct and kill themselves. Me—I was raped at twelve, and from being raped, I felt shocked. I felt scared, confused, and it changed my life. I felt I had no one to talk to, no one to help me, and no one to stop the abuser.

Then I began to think I was useless as if my "no" wasn't no and like my words didn't mean nothing at all. I then became promiscuous because men wanted to have sex, and I thought that if I said no my words wouldn't stick, so I ended up on countless days, on countless nights, going on days looking and searching for love and men when they had one agenda. And that was to put me on my back. And when they succeeded I lay underneath them, cry inside. Broken, hurt, and not understanding why I kept putting myself in the same situation with a different person, think that maybe one day he will love me. Giving my body away, not voluntary but still not saying no. The rape really affected my life.

Another thing that affected my life is that no one helped me, no one did anything. My aunt said "oh she's lying, no one believe her" and then when we were alone, she would ask me "why didn't you tell me?" "Why didn't I tell you?" You wouldn't believe me. And you put that man before me and your children" I would say. But she would just deny it. I felt like I couldn't talk to her. Like she didn't care. She was all about herself and all about money. If it was nothing to benefit her, she could care less.

My last husband was also raped as a child it was a neighborhood friend that raped him. He was playing, and the next thing he knew, he said he passed out and woke up hurting. It sounds like I run into a lot of previously raped victims or verbally abused women. I share my testimony on how I made it through. And I let them know that they can make it as well. I share some other stories that I've heard while passing through. Different apartments, cities and states. I met a lot of ... I'm not going to use the term crack head (because some of them were heroin addicts) and some of them did other forms of drugs. They open up and shared their stories with me. For some reason, people feel comfortable to share their stories. So we converse. And in most cases end up praying at the end of our conversation. Sometimes we try to hold on to our connection on another but as the years fly by we drift apart. I really miss them, the people I've came in contact with, and I wonder how their doing, holding up. What they're doing in their lives right now.

Not to be all over the place, but one thing I forgot to mention: After my aunt found out about the rape, she tried to make me feel like I was crazy, like I was lying, and like she wanted me to believe what she wanted me to believe. She would keep asking me questions trying to confuse me. Taking me back and forth to the police station. Telling me that I said something that I didn't. And telling me that I didn't say something that I did. So, I guess that she could cope with the reality of what took place. I guess that she was in denial. In disbelief, and didn't know how to handle the situation. Or rather not deal with it. Some people just act like its normal. And choose to undress it. Maybe this is one of the reasons I wanted to kill her.

Violence: Some people turn to violence from a lack of attention, mental health, or behavioral problems, or simply by being possessed by spirits. Or it could be used as a form of escape from anger, rage, or retaliation from trauma, abuse, or pain. It goes hand in hand. Basically, with the reason why some people use drugs to escape the pain, trauma or abuse. But me? I became violent because I didn't know how to communicate and release frustration. So I would blow my top—when all I had to do was communicate and speak how I felt. But no…. I kept it bottled up. I was about to become a serial killer, and didn't even know it.

I started to become a product of my environment. I became brainwashed to see thing as the world seen them. They had remote control. Controlling our actions. What we do, what we wear. How we act. What we eat. All through media. The music that we listen to. It penetrates the spirit, gets into the flesh, and allows us to create an emotion that leads to the flesh and to promiscuity, which creates a bond, soul tie, and covenant. I covered my hurt and pain with a bandage, but I had to uncover my truths so I could be healed. I guess you can say I started having sex from being hurt. Covering and masking the issues of pain. I became fighting myself, I guess. It was my spirit versus my flesh. My spirit was willing, and wanted to do what was right. But my flesh struggled with seeking something to make me feel good instead of something to heal me from the hurt and pain. I was full of brokenness. I became lost. Trying to find something in sex that was never even there. I got nothing from it but a feeling, and when it was all over, I was back feeling the way I felt. So it was just a distraction from the moment. It was a mere waste of time. I was an addict just like the crack heads that I talked about. How can I talk about them no loving themselves, or not respecting themselves, and I fell into the same category. How dare me. Same problem, different addiction. At first I blamed it on me not having self-control, but that's where God comes in at. And I have a choice.

Sex began to control my life Maybe keep this? → [[[Sex began to control my life. It all started with rape. Even though I said "no" to the rape, and I fought him off of me, the feeling of sex in itself became pleasurable. So was I wrong because I gave into the feeling?]]]

Sex before marriage

So, sleeping around, Ok let's say, "Sex before marriage". We have sex with people who we think we love. And we also think that were going to be together forever. This is what we think and very seldom some of us do. Others say its love" and it's lust. And some just don't care. They have sex because they like the feeling. Not caring about soul ties, diseases, or bringing a child into this world. Feelings of losing yourself in sex. (Note: like when you have sex so much that you stop being who you want to be just to please somebody.) Sex not only takes your energy, but your essence away. Which is a power that is special. That once is given away, it can never be replaced. Some of us have sex to fill a void, some to feed an addiction by satisfying the flesh. Like eating or whatever we do to satisfy the flesh. For every action there is a reaction. But are you willing to bear the consequences that come with the action. Some people are walking around with HIV and AIDS because they couldn't control the flesh, which we are going to call the "inner beast". A hungry demon. Remember the saying "everything that glitters isn't gold"? The devil dresses everything up to make it look desirable, pleasing, tempting to the eye, and it can be the very thing that traps you. Brings you to demise. So be careful who you keep in your company. Or who you the power to. When you're vulnerable, people take advantage of you. And you begin to form unhealthy relationships.

Journey

Writing this book, I had to relive the pain of the traumatic life events.

Topic: marriage

Do we know one another spiritually, emotionally? Because marriage is not just supposed to be physical. We're supposed to be intimate and expressing love through sharing our mind and hearts. We are married. We are to fight for one another and the spirit, and not fight each other. In marriage I've learned to trust.

Things to do in marriage:

Speak blessings over one another's lives. Go out together and have time alone. Cook for one another. Massage one another. Shower/take bathes together. Do not hid anything from one another. Don't go to bed angry. Communicate and listen. Always say "I love you". Enjoy one another. Have sex regularly. Keep yourself looking nice and smelling nice. Don't allow small things to matter. And last but not least, keep God first. Pray for one another. And any emotions, past hurts, and soul ties that were before your marriage out of your marriage. Get repentance, deliverance, and make the right choices. Live God's purpose for your lives by willing your hearts and minds to the Lord. Do not be tempted by this world. Stay obedient to Christ. Think of things you don't know about your mate: favorite color, favorite food, favorite kind of flowers, favorite sports team, favorite outings, favorite music, favorite movies, favorite TV shows,

And what makes them happy as well as angry. What attracts you to them?

Favorite hobby. (← Favorite thing), vacation spot.

116

Are you able to build an empire together? What are you goals and visions? Is your mate your priority? Do you understand the value of family? The order of household? Do you understand communication is a must? And your mate should be your best friend. Not withholding any information from your mate. You should be selfless, dependable, honest, caring, thoughtful, compassionate, respectful, giving, stable, determined, loyal, gentle, understanding, persistent, reasonable, trustworthy, confident, strong, consistent, romantic, and loving. Unconditional love is a must. Also have morals, a plan, AB and C. And your lives should be a ministry.

The man/father should be the head of household. The woman is to listen to the man, but she is free to have her own opinion. She is to follow her husband, as he follows Christ. And if he doesn't follow Christ, ladies, you're not supposed to be married to him. When in fact, or if you are, stay prayerful, because you still must listen.

Those who are single, keep God first. And he'll send you a mate. We can't pick them ourselves. We choose the wrong ones.

Definitions:

Spirit – wind, breath, essence of being. Genesis 1: 2, Luke 1: 80 evil or good spirit.

Temperance – self-control, use of a level head and sound mind. 1 Corinthians 9:25. Galatians 5:23, 2 Peter 1:3~8

Journey

Does anybody know what the word "prosecute" mean? Treated badly, harassed, and caused to suffer. Jeremiah 29:18, Matthew 5:10

Who knows what "perseverance" means? Not giving up, lasting, consistency, endurance. Ephesians 6:18

Are we able to obey God out of his love for Him? Because of Jesus dying for our sins, we now live and have life to share with others. How can most of us not even care about our life? Life to most is shoes, clothes, cars, house, and boyfriend, girlfriend, being cool, staying cool, and staying fly, sex, sex, sex, money, smoking, drinking, or how others see you. Not ever once did you think about how God was going to wipe out the entire human population, and it first started because it was then how it is now. Brothers killing brother, daughters killing mothers, parents not taking time out with their children to teach them from homosexuality. The world is falling quick, and people are coming against one another making the process quicker. We were given the freedom of choice, yes, but why not choose Jesus—He chose you.

Power of words/The Word:

Let's stop complaining and murmuring about the things that does not matter. Try to make every situation a positive one. Looking at the bright side of a bad thing. Don't speak everything you think. Because when you complain you remain. Keep a good attitude. There is power in your words. The word of God says to acknowledge him all of your ways, and He will direct your path. Keep your mind on forgiving and repenting. God wants all of our attention.

Speak words of affirmation. (Definition) Affirmation is encouragement to yourself. Speaking life into your situation out loud on a daily basis. Claim salvation and victory, overcome the enemy. If you speak negative about you, or others, you are affirming the word of the enemy. Quote the word of God. "Faith cometh by hearing and hearing by the word of God." Romans 10:17. "Life and death are in the power of the tongue." Proverbs 18:21 your words can kill or nourish.

Repeat after me: *"I realize I have received Jesus as my Lord and Savior, and I believe he receives me. My body is a temple for the Holy Spirit to dwell. I am redeemed, cleaned, healed, delivered, and set free. Sanctified by the blood of Christ. Satan has no place in me, no power over my life, no unsettle claims against me. Through the blood of Jesus, I crucify my flesh, myself, my ego, and my ways to become more like God. I love you, Lord.*

No weapon formed against me shall prosper. I desire to walk in the Spirit and not fulfill the lust of the flesh. Not doing things of this world. I thank you, Lord for wisdom, knowledge, power, authority, and control over the enemy. Thank you for your mercy, grace, healing, kindness, love, patience, presence, promises, protection, purpose, salvation, strength, and wisdom. In Jesus name, Amen."

Journey

Love descriptions

Can't go a day without seeing your face.
- When you allow your heart to lead instead of your brain.
- When words can't even describe your feelings. When you say, "I love you.", and it still feel unexpressed.
- When you can talk to your mate without using words.
- When you feel like it's a crush.
- When you can tell by the actions alone.
- Let's not forget from the look in their eyes.
- True love makes a sacrifice.
- To feel like you're floating in thin air.
- Butterflies in your belly.
- Surrounded by stars
- When you smile for no reason at all because your mate is around.
- How a room feel like it spinning with your feet not on the ground.
- When your body feels empty when they're not around.
- When they inspire you with your hopes and dreams.
- Holding hands, sharing fears, anxieties, aspirations.
- Introduce you to family and friends.
- When you know that you wouldn't trade them for nothing in the world.
- When you give up everything to just be with them.
- When all that matters in their happiness.
- When you hear their voice, you get excited.

- When you still can become shy around them.
- When your heart skips beats, or beats faster, when they say your name.
- When your body melts every time they touch you.
- When everything makes you of them.
- When you can't imagine life without them.
- When you *can* imagine spending every day with them.
- When you can play like kids and enjoy one another.

Love is being with a person if they are down and out or busted. To love a person is not because of what they have, it's because of who they are. Not what they can do for you.

Dad

A lot of little girls grow up happy with a father. Having this happy feeling of being daddy's angel. Daddy's little girl. I've hoped to wander how one day it would feel. But I'm happy for them, though. "All I need is my mom." That's what I've always told myself. Not being happy, I couldn't control myself. After she left me, she was gone. Me traveling the streets, finding many homes, and the many different things I put myself through trying to experience life. Jesus is also true. Because too been through what I have been to know what I've been through. It's up to me to tell the world "God, I'll be true to you. I give my life to you. I am a sinner full of sin. So dirty. Filthy. Unto you, o Lord, that I may dwell and your presence and be used for your glory. You, I will trust. Too much is given, much is required. I'm ready for you Lord. I'll follow your guidance, your will, and I will finish your assignments. Just leave me with your guidance. I will lift you up, and praise you, o God. I will exalt your name, and let people know who you are.

Journey

My heavenly father, you've always showed me the way. You've loved me, and continue to send me through. Even today. Thank you, Lord. My Father, my provider, my love… you provided me with earthly fathers. Father figures. A step dad. Uncles, grandfather, great grandfather, spiritual father, as well as a natural father. And even though he has not been present, he still created me. So thank you all for pouring into my life love, happiness, and good memories. I truly love you all with all of my heart. I thank God for placing you all in my life to fulfill the purpose God had given them for me.

Looking for the love I lost

The love I experienced from having a mother was like no other love. Someone to bandage your boo-boos, wipe your tears, give unconditional love, encourage you, nurture you, and simply have your back. I lost my mom at 34. She was 34, of course. I was only twelve. It took a toll on me, but I didn't show quick reaction. I began trying to find a replacement in men, but only found disappointment from being used and taken advantage of. They lied to me to get me in bed, but led me to believe that we would be together forever, and they possessed the traits that I once received for my mom. Over and over again. Man after man. Lie after lie. Tear I was cry. Until one day I decided not to have a heart. I decided to play the game they played.

I learned the game first handedly from my uncles. They tricked, played, and manipulated women, so I started to do it to guys.

I would make them fall in love and wouldn't give a rat's tail about them. At first, I guess you can say, I wanted to hurt them how they hurt me. Then I started to use men for sex. It gave me experience and I became darned well at it. It was like a competition to me. And it drove them crazy. I learned how to use my body in different ways. That had them crawling back for more. Until one day I had a one night stand. And I thought everything would be cool. This man stalked me. I moved out of state to Michigan. And came back to visit, and this man sat outside of my grandmother's house. One night. I took the bus to 71st and Dorchester, and walked across the train tracks, around the school—to my grandma's house in Chicago. I didn't notice his car. She had two locks on her storm door, and two locks on her front door. By the time I got the first lock unlocked, he was standing clear behind me. He startled me, but I didn't want him to know I was scared, so I acted like everything was cool. He asked me to sit in the car, so he could talk to me. So I walked to the car with him because his hand was on my back pushing me to the car. I got in the car, and he asked me, "Hey, where you been? I've been calling you and trying to reach you."

I said, "I don't live here. I moved away."

He then asked me for sex, which I told him I was unable to do because I was bleeding, but he didn't care.

I had on a tampon. This man crawled over to the passenger side of the car. I can't remember what I had on, but I know he was able to get to my privates. He chocked me until I was unable to breath. Only tears came out of my eyes. He had sex with me in his car. After I told him I didn't want to have sex with him. It was like being 12 all over again. Being raped. When he finished, I went inside the house, walked up to my room crying. Feeling hurt and dirty. I called my sister and told her, she told me to come back home. She meant Detroit. I also told my cousin Suga, and she wanted him dead. She wanted to help me take him out. We had a plan to go get a gun from my uncle's house and shoot him up at the mall, where he worked. But God ministered to me, telling me to let Him deal with it. So I did.

This was one of the things that slowed me down having sex and playing with men. Another was me getting married.

First Marriage

I got married for all the wrong reasons. First reason was to get away from my aunt and from being a mom to my aunt's children. So, I seen a guy on the bus. Asked, "Hey, do you want some skittles?" in which he totally ignored me, blaming it on his headphones. So I followed him to the back of the bus. He took his headphones off, and I presented the question again, "Would you like some skittles?" He said, "No.". So I asked for his phone number and realized I was on the wrong bus. So I gathered up the children and got off the bus. I wasn't going to call him. Almost a month went by before I actually did. And I only called to invite him to Thanksgiving dinner. I invited my ex as well, and a few other friends. Just because I knew that they weren't doing anything for the holiday. So, needless to say, it was a total wreck with my ex being there and all. One of my friends tried to talk to my ex-husband (which was my friend at the time), but I got kind of annoyed. We end up dating from November to Valentine's Day. Then started discussing marriage as a plan to get away. May 21st, 2004, we got married. Ten days after my 18th birthday. And then, not long after, I moved to Detroit.

When I moved to Detroit, I thought to myself, "A new life". I lived with my sister's mom, my sister, four brothers, and my uncle. It was all of us in a two bedroom house. When my dad got out of jail, he moved in as well. When he came, he had an agenda of his own.

He pawed me off to a drug dealer. Thank God the dealer didn't want to have sex with me or hurt me. You maybe be thinking to yourself, "Wow, her dad pawed her off.", but my dad was on drugs heavily. Not giving an excuse for him pawning me off, but I know drugs make you do things you wouldn't usually do. The drug dealer just wanted to feel loved. Go out on dates, go shopping, have somebody to talk to. However he did ask me if he could give oral fixation, and I said ok. He was really nice to me, but I fell in love with a waiter when we were out on a date. He wasn't even our waiter. He walked past and I felt dizzy. Like I was flying through space, and I didn't know why. For one reason or another, I end up back in Chicago visiting, and my visit became a short stay. (Maybe for like a couple months). In this time, I moved in with my husband. We were going to the grocery store, running errands, and cleaning the house. Like a normal family. Him not knowing that I was leaving again. My husband was deeply in love with me, but I looked at him as family. Was never able to fall in love with him. But he was my best friend, but he couldn't understand if we were married why I didn't act like it. Some nights I didn't come home, I stayed at my grandmother's house or friend's house. I never called him or checked in. I guess that's how I got kidnapped.

This is what happened: I met a guy, and he seemed nice. I trusted him, and he made a stop at his house. I asked to use the bathroom, and he locked me in his house. I was unable to get out for like a week. So he wouldn't hurt me, I acted as though things were cool. I didn't have a cell phone, didn't know where I was at, I just knew that we were on the third floor with bars on the windows, bars on the doors, and a double-sided lock. You couldn't get in or out without a key. And he did any and everything he wanted to do me in that week. And then he let me go. I look through the house when he left. I grabbed a piece of paper with his name on it to report him, but the paper that I grabbed was a doctor's statement saying this man had chlamydia and gonorrhea. So guess who also had chlamydia and gonorrhea. I did, but didn't know at that time. I end up sleeping with my husband, and went back to Michigan, slept with my boyfriend, and they both got it. And then I went to the hospital to find out that I had it and had to get a shot and take medicine. Both guys called me and told me that they had it. I thought that I gave it to them. Well, I did, but only because of the guy that kidnapped me passing it to me.

I became a stripper. One day I rode to Dejavu to pick up his cousin. When I see the sign "Amateur Night", so I asked, "What is amateur night?" and she said "when you audition to work here", so I said that I wanted to do it.

I came back and did amateur night, and I got a little over 500 dollars from two songs. So, 500 versus 0 was a lot. I decided to start working at the club, but most night I would go home crying because of the image I was portraying. Looking in the mirrors, looking at my body in the nude, and how men seen me on the stage, throwing cash, and starring with eyes of lust. It just made me feel horrible. Some of the girls asked in the dressing room, "Hey, you ok? What's up?" and I said, "No, I don't want to do this. I can't do this." One lady said, "Have a drink. It'll be alright. Think of yourself dancing at home in a mirror by yourself. Or dancing in front of your guy." I said "Ok, and took the drink." I started to drink and smoke to work at the bar.

Journey

But each night that I worked, I made between twelve and fifteen hundred bucks. When the other women got wind of this, I started to have problems. I guess I was taking money from them, but as a dancer, I didn't see myself as a dancer. I see myself as a performer on a Broadway play acting a part. Just in the nude! I would hip hop dance, break dance, footwork, and pop drop and shake it. But with each song I told a story, I had props, I felt that I should take the show to Vegas and become a Las Vegas showgirl. I just never made it to Vegas. Working at the club became dangerous. Strippers was coming up missing. Being found dead in trucks of cars. It was a shame. Some of them had children. But I guess that's what comes with meeting people outside of the club. This life was crazy. And a bit scary. But I had my sister with me, my boyfriend, my boyfriend's brother, and his cousin. They all looked out for me, so I wasn't alone. Some guys at the bar, which were customers, tried to take me home on different occasions. I refused and I end up home safe. I caught myself a few times ministering to the strippers. I know they looked at me like "Hey! You doing the same thing!", but I told them, "I won't be here for long."

Why didn't I think to save the money, I don't know. I gave it all away. I felt it was dirty money, easy money, and I didn't really want it. I used it to buy clothes, get my hair did, go out to eat, and pay for everyone's everything. I was being used by everybody: family, so-called "friends", and my boyfriend. When I decided to stop stripping, my husband came back. He decided he wanted to make it work. So, I made plans to move back to Chicago. We tried it for a year, but he just couldn't remain faithful. But then again, neither could I. I was madly in love with the guy in Michigan, and I guess my husband felt that. We were back and forth, on and off for ten years. Then we finally got a divorce.

My second marriage

I wanted to kill myself. But not only did I want to, I tried ten times in this marriage. At first I felt like the most beautiful woman in this world, his everything, he was so loving, compassionate, loyal, caring, considerate, gentleman. But I guess it was all just an act. He became so self-centered, selfish, mean, and inconsiderate. He'd rather watch TV than to talk, hold me, or just spend time together. He started being sneaky, and making me feel like crap. How did I go from being the most desirable, wanted, loving human being to a lump of crap? I'm still trying to figure that out.

It hurt me to my soul. I tried slitting my wrists, I tried to jump out on the freeway two or three times while he was driving, which scared the crap out of him. Tried stabbing myself in the stomach. Tried to jump off the third floor balcony. I tried to run into traffic to get hit by an eighteen-wheeler semi, but he stopped me every time. I didn't feel loved, appreciated, or like I should even be here. I wanted to end it all. The only reason I didn't is because God told me "long suffering, bear the cross" at that time, I couldn't understand and all I wanted was to die. He showed me my purpose, and I couldn't take the easy way out.

Divorce hurt just as bad. I didn't think it would, being that we weren't married long, and the fact that he cheated on me. I thought I could just forget about him. However, I couldn't because being with him was the happiest--well one of the happiest, times of my life. I couldn't forget him. I don't blame him, he just wasn't strong enough.

People that I've come across

Journey

I met a lot of people, different faces, different places, and different races. But all of them had different hurts, different problems, they opened up to me at grocery stores, schools, parking lots, churches, walking through neighborhoods. No matter where I'm at, or what I'm doing, someone either stops me or I greet them, and pour out love onto them. And the stories I get in return, are crazy. Well, maybe just amazing and different because we all have stories. We all been through something.

I've met crackheads, heroin addicts, prostitutes, killers, orphans, homeless people, rape victims, loveless people, victims of hurt and defeat, and others. But they all felt comfortable enough to share their lives with me. I talked to them about God, invited them out to church, and helped anyway I could. If it was to give a hug, information, food, money, or shelter, I did. And I'm not saying this to make myself look good, but it's to show us how we should be. We should help if we can. I do it because they need it, and I have a good heart. Not to be praised, I don't walk around on the streets, "Hey, I just helped this person." We should all try loving on random people with God's love, with God's heart. Pray for someone other than your family or friends. Let's help someone else, even if it's our enemies. Let's forgive and give. We shouldn't worry about what we can get from someone. Or what they can do for us. When we change our perception on life, and just give more without wanting anything in return, and we do the work of the Lord, we will become blessed. We won't have a need or a want. All of our needs will be met because we're simply not thinking about them, but thinking about others that can't do for themselves. This is the true work of the Lord. Not worrying about our situations, our life, our pain, our past, our future, our problems, but the lady with the children, and no place to live, or the man under the bridge with no food. You know, people you see every day. And you pass by them. Stop and be a representation of Christ. Show them the love of God, don't just tell them about it. Allow them to experience it.

Some rapes happen by family members or friends or someone who we're familiar with. It can be at any time, any place. Male or female.

I really hope you enjoyed reading about my journey. Every word that I wrote was true and from my heart it took me over four years to complete this assignment. I will have apart two it was just too much to put in one book. As well as to much that happened to me all together and putting the pages together has been so overwhelming. I hope I was able to keep you interested enough to finish it and get something out of it. What I got out of living the life that I lived on this journey, was to be more caring, compassionate, loving, to be a giver, to pay more attention in life period and to follow Gods will for my life. It was fun living in sin but I'm glad that I didn't die in my mess I got the chance to get it right and ask for forgiveness. Some people die and don't make it out of the dangerous situations that I put myself in they are not even here to talk about it. I'm so thankful for God's grace over my life he had mercy over me because I know that I messed up big time. So I hope by reading this it wasn't just for entertainment or just to give your ideas or to make you feel like the things that I was doing was cool because they wasn't and I was playing with God. I told my testimony to give God glory and to tell you what not to do. I was lost in this world and acting a fool. Since I've came back to God I've been so blessed, healed, set free, delivered. I can't imagine my life without him. Everything work together for my good I have supernatural increase and a lot of miracles signs and supernatural events take place in my life I can't even began to explain. The only advice that I could give you if you're not living right is to try God whole hardly give God you're all sacrifice everything and he will give you more. And one last thing if your ever able to go to Detroit or if you live in Detroit stop in on a word in action service this will be a service that you have never ever experienced you will know you're in the house of God feel his presence and your life will never ever be the same if you don't take my word try it for yourself for a real experience with God like no other I'm not knocking no other churches, just get there.

I just want to take this time to tell you about how I found my church home and why my leaders mean so much to me. When I was still married to my 1st husband on the verge of divorce he end up moving to Detroit and decided to work it out we went from church to church to church until we got tired of going to different churches some churches played church some was not of God and some had a level of anointing that was faint so my husband decided to stop going and chill at home to praise and worship me becoming frustrated I did the same and one day I needed some hair from the beauty supply store and so I walked from Mcnickles and Wyoming down Wyoming to 7mile and on the way back home I walked through the old social security office which was now a church I looked at it from the lot and a lady came out and invited me in this day changed my life forever when I walked into the church and I didn't know what to expect but I felt the presence of God immediately after going through the doors I went to the sanctuary and fell to my knees in repentance I never been in a place that you didn't have to usher or beg God to come in he was already there at that moment alone I knew this was home and I had to be here so I rushed home to tell my husband about how amazing this place was it was Gods house and it could save our marriage not knowing at the time that the ministry really did save and restore marriages I went home to talk to him but he wasn't moved nor convinced so I started to go alone until I got tired and moved away back to Chicago but the church stayed on my heart and I had to get back to Detroit. I never been to a church that didn't gossip or form cliques or groups at word in actions. they are truly a family they move in a unit events as a whole graduations baby showers birthdays kid events barbeques you name it the entire church will attend I love that and the do it in love God moves through word in action and my leaders just thinking about them takes my breath away they are truly Gods people they showed me how to become a woman of God a lady and being a part of W.I.A. saved my life and the glory that s on this man and woman of God you have to see for yourself a lot of people say to me oh you praise them no I praise God but I honor them and I love them and I'm thankful that God thought enough about me to give me his best bishop clearance Langston and pastor Robyn Langston my jewels This man and woman took me in and loved me as their own didn't judge me but they corrected me and showed me how to get it right by being living examples not just people that told others what to do and didn't do it themselves they live it isn't nothing phony or fake about them and I don't care what anyone thinks or have to say contrary to the way I see them I know them and they live in my heart I have never met people like them ever.

Journey

    This book is about my life from the ages of 12 to 24; telling you the ways in which I had to survive and all the things I've been through in my life. Being on my own when my mother died, looking for love and affection in men-becoming pregnant at the age of 12. Not long after being raped, beat and mistreated by family. Running from place to pillowcase stripping finding love, being hurt by People whom I thought I could trust learning that I couldn't trust no one but God and how he was in my corner when no one else was. And how I could have been killed so in many different ways different times that I put myself in situations. This book will help you or someone in your family it was made to heal and deliver my story God's glory.

    Crystal Evans, bestselling author of the book Journey. A Chicago native, born to La Tisa Harding. She loves working with children, and a former teacher, passion to give love and inspiration as well as to encourage others to reach their full potential. She loves to sing, praise God, praise dance. She wants to do plays, and films of her book. Her other passion is to go into high schools and talk to the youth. Be successful in her landscaping business, construction business/contracting, open child day care facilities and adult care facilities, as well as care for the elderly. And let's not forget she wants to give back to the community by having a program where she builds confidence, by giving hair style cuts for men, women and children, who cannot afford to have it done. She wants to make them feel special. Do fashion shows and feed those without food. She loves football, favorite team Green Bay Packers. She loved playing football as a child. Her favorite colors are EARTH tone colors,

Journey

green, orange, brown, and red the same as her mother, she loves to play pool, shoot darts, and video games. Also, her favorite basketball teams are the Lakers and the Pistons. She loves to go to live games she loves to sing and dance favorite music neo-soul and oldies us not forget gospel she wants a vending truck so that she can cook and travel while selling her book.

Made in the USA
Middletown, DE
01 June 2015